My Brother's Keeper

A PERSONAL NARRATIVE ABOUT COPING WITH THE LOSS OF A SIBLING

DR. EBONY N. ERVIN

Cover Design: Ebony N. Ervin via Photo Lab (VicMan LLC)
Interior Design: Ebony N. Ervin

ISBN: 978-1-0991-4831-6

First Edition, June 2019

In loving memory of my brother and best friend,

Jason Tremaine Ervin

Erv, I hope I've made you proud.
#LongLiveKingErv

CONTENTS

INTRODUCTION

Upon losing my brother, Jason, I visited a major book retailer in the hopes of finding some literature on coping with the loss of a sibling. After skimming the shelves, I found there were many self-help books available to help people cope with the loss of a loved one: the loss of a parent, the loss of a child, the loss of a spouse – even the loss of a pet. However, I was unable to find much literature on coping with the loss of an adult sibling, especially a sibling who was of a young age or specifically, a younger sibling.

The loss of a sibling is unique when compared to the loss of any other immediate blood relative (parent or child). It is even more unique if the lost sibling is a younger one. Being the older sibling means you've had a relationship with this person since their birth. In theory, this relationship will be retained for a longer period than the parent-child relationship and vice versa. In fact, under normal circumstances, the sibling relationship will be the longest relationship of *any* kind.

When a person loses a sibling, he or she must cope with a loss of both the past and the future. In other words, there is grief associated with the siblings' past life together, and there is grief for what should have been the siblings' relationship in the future. Once this relationship or bond has been broken by this sort of tragedy, it can never be repaired or replaced. Thus, leaving an eternal void in the surviving sibling's heart.

These characteristics, in part, motivated me to write this book – to share my story, my experience, and my insight – on coping with the loss of my beloved brother. Writing this book proved to be a very emotional experience. Consequently, I found myself writing a great bit of it with a heavy heart and in between tears. However, I found it to have a therapeutic effect as well. As I often found myself smiling and laughing just as much, if not more than, I cried – and for that I am grateful.

My hope is that if you are reading this book in an effort to help cope with the loss of your sibling, it in some way helps you as well. At the very least, upon reading my personal story, I hope you are reminded of the precious memories and loving moments spent with your sibling. Remember, your recollections have the power to supersede time. Thus, remaining with you until you see your loved one again.

Alternatively, if you are not the person experiencing the loss but know someone who has, I believe you too will be enlightened and inspired by my story.

THE MEMORIES OF THE PAST

Chapter 1: The Early Years

*• **keep·er** /kēpər/ – (noun) a person who manages
or looks after something or someone.*[*]

From the moment our parents brought my brother, Jason, home from the hospital, I have been my brother's keeper – especially with us being so close in age and with it only being the two of us. I was born September 12, 1984, and Jason was born September 10, 1986, making us almost exactly two years apart. Interestingly enough, our mom had planned to have her second cesarean on September 12th, my birthday, but Jason came a couple days early. I guess he needed his own day.

Being my new little brother's keeper, I made it my duty to alert my mom any time the baby was crying. My mom described one instance where I obviously didn't feel she was answering his cry fast enough, because soon after he began to cry, she looked upstairs, and there I was, dragging Jason on the floor to her! You see, even back then, I wasn't going to let my baby brother cry, want, or hurt for a moment longer than he had to. Not if it was in any way under my control.

Fast forward two to three years later, at the age when most children begin talking to other kids and adults, Jason didn't. This

---

[*] As defined by the Google online dictionary.

initially alarmed our parents. But after seeking medical attention, they were told nothing was seriously wrong with him.

As his sister, I knew all along nothing was seriously wrong with Jason, because he had no problem talking to me. In fact, at one of our doctor visits, when the pediatrician asked Jason what was wrong, instead of him responding to her, my mom said he looked at me, and I answered on his behalf.

The doctor responded: *"Well, there's your problem right there! He's not talking because she's doing all the talking for him. If you manage to shut her up, maybe he'll start talking."* (To this day, I am not convinced I was a part of the problem.)

As small kids, Jason often followed in my footsteps, which wasn't always a good thing. I still laugh when I think about a story my mom once shared about the two of us: She had taken us to visit some of our older relatives. Prior to entering their home, she warned us that their house might *"smell a little funny,"* but we were instructed not to say anything about it. Being the obedient children that we were, we agreed.

After a few moments of being in the house, however, my mom looked at the two us and was quickly appalled and embarrassed, because Jason and I were pinching our noses! And knowing the two of us, I'm sure I pinched my nose first, and Jason subsequently followed suit. In my mind, I figured out an alternate solution to the problem. Even at a young age, I was smart like that. My mom said not to *say* anything. She didn't say not to *do* anything.

Now, although it may seem like I was a bit of a troublemaker back then, I don't agree. I think Jason was just saving his voice and actions for later, because as we got older, our personalities reversed. I became more quiet and introverted while Jason became more outspoken and extroverted.

This became evident while we were still young children. I could often be found alone, perhaps reading a book or completing a jigsaw puzzle. Being as such, our parents didn't necessarily have to keep their eyes on me, because chances were, I wasn't up to too much.

Jason, on the other hand, was the polar opposite. Our parents *constantly* had to watch him. If they let him roam free for even a few minutes, he could (and would) find something to climb on or get into. He loved to climb the kitchen cabinets or to open the dishwasher and use it as a step to reach things on the countertop.

Better yet, this story was so unbelievable that it made the local newspaper: One day, Jason (age two or three) and my dad were outside, and for some reason one of the car doors was left open. My dad turned away for a minute, and before he knew it, Jason had managed to climb into the car; somehow knocked the car into gear; and went riding into the neighbor's yard! When my dad reached the car, he said Jason was sitting in it (unharmed) laughing. He obviously enjoyed the ride.

It didn't take long for Jason to become more vocal either. And not only did he begin to talk more, but he also developed a bit of a potty mouth. This occurred as a result of our grandmother (our dad's mom) babysitting us. She would tend to curse from time to time, and like most small kids do, Jason would repeat the things he heard most often.

He would say things to our parents like: *"Close the damn door!"* or, *"Sit your a** down!"* Eventually, he learned certain words were "bad words" that weren't to be repeated, and his potty mouth became clean again – at least temporarily.

Nonetheless, Jason and I always remained close despite our differing personalities. It was simply how we were raised. Our parents always showered both of us with love and adoration, but it was our dad who raised us to know and understand the value of family. He taught us to not only love each other as brother and sister, but to always be best friends to one another. As a result, growing up, if you knew one of us, more than likely you knew the other – not only because we were siblings, but also because we were best friends.

Chapter 2: The Adolescent Years

"Train up a child in the way he should go,
and when he is old he will not depart from it."
(Proverbs 22:6[*])

The idea that mother's *raise* their daughters but *love* their sons definitely held true in our household – or at least from my vantage point it did. I felt as though I was brought up to be the "responsible" one, both inside and outside the home. In hindsight, this could've simply been because I was the oldest.

As a child, however, I never understood why I had chores outside of cleaning my room – for example: dusting, loading the dishwasher, or sweeping and mopping the kitchen floor. Whereas Jason was never required to do any similar tasks or respective chores, such as taking out the trash or mowing the lawn. In fact, when Jason got his first job (fast food), I remember him calling home to ask my mom how to sweep and mop! That will forever be the initial proof that I was raised, and Jason was loved.

Despite our differing domestic expectations, however, Jason and I both excelled in grade school and junior high. We were always on the Honor Roll and received an award for perfect attendance almost every year. My scholastic achievements continued into my high school years, whereas Jason's grades became more average – not

---

[*] From the New King James Version (NKJV).

because he wasn't capable, but more so because he developed other interests.

He started playing football and began spending more time outside of class with his friends and teammates. He was also a bit of a class clown and became known for his comedic personality. I was also involved in extracurricular activities in high school – the marching band, student government association, and Girl Scouts to name a few – but receiving good grades was always my priority. According to Jason (and probably to you too at this point), I was a nerd.

Jason and I both attended college after graduating high school. I opted to go away to Stillman College (Tuscaloosa, AL), while Jason chose to stay in our hometown (Huntsville, AL) and attend Alabama A&M University, our mother's alma mater. Despite my going away, Jason and I remained close throughout my four years at Stillman. We would talk on the phone several times a week, and I would come home every other weekend and during school breaks.

Jason would occasionally visit me in Tuscaloosa as well. He'd also come down for our annual Homecoming festivities each year. It wasn't long before the people I associated with – friends, sorority sisters, and dormmates[*] – knew who he was. Just like in high school and years prior, to know one of us, usually meant knowing both of us.

Jason never finished at Alabama A&M University. Although he had done well his freshman year, by his sophomore year, his grades had begun to slip as his attendance became less and less. He had lost interest in the Computer Science degree he had been pursuing and,

---

[*] I pledged the Epsilon Eta Chapter of Delta Sigma Theta Sorority, Inc. in the spring of 2004…oo-oop!

instead, had developed an interest in music. He didn't return to college after his second year.

Jason and I both began working during high school at the age of fifteen. We were both hired at a local Subway restaurant. From there, I went on to work in retail during breaks and following my freshman and sophomore years at Stillman. However, during the summer following my junior year, I began interning for an aerospace and defense technology company named Northrop Grumman (Huntsville).

Although the intern pay was great at Northrop Grumman, I wasn't completely sold on the idea of becoming an engineer upon graduation. As a result, I obtained a part-time job as a pharmacy technician at a local pharmacy during my senior year at Stillman. Jason worked in the fast-food industry during and after his time at Alabama A&M, initially at a McDonalds and later at a Jersey Mikes.

Around this time, Jason had also made some new friends and had begun making music. He created songs by himself, as a solo artist (hip-hop/rap), and with his friends as an r&b/hip-hop group. Eventually a local carpet company chain, Rock Bottom Carpets, asked them to create a jingle for their company. I remember Jason and his friends (and myself) being so excited to hear their jingle on the radio for the first time.

During my final semester at Stillman, I was offered a position as a Systems Engineer at Northrup Grumman. The position was full-time and came with a salary of $50,000 per year. Based on my internship experience, however, I ultimately knew that engineering was not the career path I wanted to pursue.

Nonetheless, I accepted the position. After all, *"my mama didn't raise no fool!"* But because I knew engineering was not for me, I also applied to pharmacy school during my last year at Stillman. I loved working in the pharmacy as a technician and could see myself as a pharmacist one day.

I graduated summa cum laude from Stillman in 2006 with a Bachelor of Science in Mathematics. Upon graduating, however, I still had not been accepted into pharmacy school. Instead, I had been wait-listed at both schools in which I had applied.[*]

However, within a week or two of graduation, I received an acceptance letter from my first choice: Mercer University in Atlanta, GA. Yet and still, I continued working at Northrop Grumman that summer. Additionally, I transferred my pharmacy tech position to a location in Huntsville and was working there part-time, at night or on the weekends.

When I informed my parents and boyfriend, Rob, that I planned to leave Northrup Grumman at the end of the summer to attend pharmacy school, I received major push-back from both parties.[†] I understood their reservations. My parents had grown up a lot less fortunate than me and Jason. Therefore, walking away from a $50,000 salary seemed irrational in their eyes. And with most students not having jobs in their field upon graduation, Rob didn't want me to turn my back on such a great opportunity.

---

[*] Being placed on the wait list meant that although I had not initially been accepted into the upcoming class, if for some reason a person who *was* accepted decided not to attend, depending on how high I was on the wait list, I could be accepted in their place. Otherwise, I would have to reapply for the following year's class.

[†] Name (Rob) has been changed.

As a potential compromise, my parents suggested that I stay at Northrup Grumman for at least a year; save some money; and if I was still interested in becoming a pharmacist after a year, to reapply at that time. (Rob offered a similar suggestion.) Jason, on the other hand, told me to make whatever decision I felt was best for me, and if that was quitting my job to go to pharmacy school, *"then do it."*

I decided to take Jason's advice. I had to strike while the iron was hot. I knew the chance of me going, or even being accepted, into pharmacy school after working for a year was slim to none. (In hindsight, I'm pretty sure my parents knew that too.) So about three weeks before classes began at Mercer, I put in my two-week's notice and resigned from Northrop Grumman.

Chapter 3: The Religious Background

*"...But as for me and my house,
we will serve the Lord."*
(Joshua 24:15[*])

Jason and I were part of a pious family and raised in a Christian household. We attended Progressive Union Missionary Baptist Church (Huntsville, AL) and spent most Sunday mornings attending worship service. As youths, Jason and I, were very active in the church. We served on the junior usher board, sang in the choir, and took part in many of the activities and functions offered by Progressive Union. As adolescents, we both gave our lives to Christ and were baptized.

Jason and I both became less active in the church upon graduating high school. He rarely attended church with our parents once I went away to college, and I never searched for a temporary church home while in Tuscaloosa. Although the four of us would attend church more frequently when I was home for summer breaks or during the holidays, we would seldom go when I visited for the weekend during the school year – primarily because I would often be traveling back to Tuscaloosa on Sunday mornings.

When I graduated from Stillman and moved back home for the summer, I began attending church again more frequently. Jason, however, was reluctant to do so. As a young adult, he had begun to

[*] From the New King James Version (NKJV).

feel that church service was "boring." An even bigger issue to him was the fact that he didn't like dressing up. In particular, he didn't like wearing what he described as "church shoes."

Instead, Jason, preferred to wear his Jordan sneakers. It got to the point where my parents would practically beg him to go to church with us. I was convinced my mom begged because she really wanted him to go, but my dad only begged because he didn't want my mom to be upset. You know the saying: *"Happy wife. Happy life."*

Eventually Jason and our parents reached a "compromise" about him attending church: He could wear his Jordan's, but he still had to wear a button-up style shirt and a nice pair of pants. Initially Jason was content with this agreement, but over time the clothing requirement fell by the wayside as well. Jason's argument to my mom was that God didn't care what he wore to church, so why should she?

Now, I'm not sure if my mom gave up on Jason's church attire because he had a valid point, or because she was desperate for him to attend church with us. Although I suspect it was a tad bit of both. Nonetheless, going forward, when the four of us would attend church together, Jason would have on a polo-style shirt, jeans, and a fresh pair of Jordan's.

Despite the decline in our church attendance as young adults, I want to make it clear that Jason and I never stopped believing in God, praying, or being thankful for our blessings during that time. We had no problems stating we were Christians. We were proud members of Progressive Union Missionary Baptist Church. And we were happy to say we'd given our lives to Christ and had been baptized.

THE CIRCUMSTANCES OF THE PRESENT

Chapter 4: The Pharmacist vs. The Chef

"You may be as different as the sun and the moon,
but the same blood flows through both your hearts…"
– George R.R. Martin

I moved to Atlanta during the summer of 2006 to attend
pharmacy school. I had been accepted into Mercer University, where I
would be pursuing a Doctor of Pharmacy degree (a four-year
program).

Soon after I moved, Jason and his friends began visiting the
city quite often. There weren't many opportunities for up and coming
music artists in Huntsville, so they would come to Atlanta to perform
at different open mics and talent shows. They eventually signed a
contract with a local management company and began visiting the city
on a routine basis.

Because Jason was coming to the city so often, I suggested that
he move to Atlanta and live with me. Since he had dropped out of
college by this time, I encouraged him to move not only to pursue his
musical dreams and aspirations, but also (and more importantly) to
pursue a career as a culinarian.

Jason eventually took heed to my advice and moved to Atlanta
in 2008, after being accepted into the culinary arts program at Le
Cordon Bleu College of Culinary Arts Atlanta (an 18-month program).
Two of his best friends and fellow musicians, Reuben and Matthew
(Reu and Matt for short), moved to Atlanta soon after he did. The

three of them were like brothers, and that's exactly how Jason referred to them – "my brothers."

Jason and I both ended up graduating in the spring of 2010. Although I had originally planned to stay in Atlanta upon graduation, I ended up accepting a pharmacist position in Huntsville and thus moved back home. Jason, however, decided to stay in Atlanta upon finishing culinary school. He had fallen in love with the fast pace of the city. Plus, since Reu and Matt were there, he also stayed to continue pursuing his musical endeavors.

After living and practicing pharmacy in Huntsville for about a year and a half, I decided I wanted to move back to Atlanta. I made plans to complete the requirements for Georgia pharmacist licensure in the beginning of 2012 and had my pharmacist position transferred later that year. Because I ultimately wanted to live in Atlanta long-term, I decided not to rent housing when I moved. Instead, I immediately began the home-buying process – living in Jason's one-bedroom apartment for a few months, sleeping on his couch until I closed on my home.

Since I knew Jason (or Erv, as I usually called him) would be moving in with me upon the termination of his lease, I only considered homes with either a finished basement or separate living spaces, so both of us could have our privacy. I remember my realtor calling late one evening:

"Hey, I know it's late, but I wanna show you this property. I think it's exactly what you've been looking for. It's really nice, so I know it won't be on the market for long. Are you available to come see it?"

Luckily, I was off from work. And since Erv was also home, I talked him into riding with me to view the property. This was the only home he visited throughout my entire house-hunting process.

Everything about the home seemed perfect: the price, the build, and the location (Stone Mountain). The home had three levels including a finished basement, which would serve as Erv's space. The upstairs area would then be my space. And we'd share the main level in between, which housed the kitchen and living spaces. I told my realtor I wanted to make an offer and on December 14, 2012, at the age of 28, I became a homeowner!

Jason was 26 when he moved into the house. At that time, I told him he was free to live with me until he turned 30. I figured by age 30, he would be in a financial position to live on his own. Although I gave him a few bills to be responsible for each month (because the only place he could live for free was with our parents), he was still able to save a little each pay period. Well, depending on what pair of Jordan's were being released that weekend.

Family Ties

- **The Two of Us**

When Jason moved into the house, the bond between us grew even stronger. We would hangout, watch TV, talk, and laugh all the time – like best friends. In fact, Erv would always talk to me like I was one of his homeboys versus his sister, or a girl. Also, his childhood potty mouth returned. It was nothing for him to swear. He didn't mean any ill will, harm, or disrespect by his vulgarities. It was just simply the way he talked.

Jason was known as the family comedian and *always* kept me laughing. He could literally find the humor in any situation, regardless of how trivial or how serious. For example, when he finally decided to shave his head bald, he not only went to the barber shop every week to maintain his precious beard, but also spent extra time shaving at home, making sure there was no stubble on his scalp. I remember teasing him about the length of time he spent in the mirror shaving. His response: *"Instead of laughin', yo a** need to be payin' attention! Takin' some notes! For when yo a** go bald!"* – lol.

In another instance, I had been feeling down and depressed for several days. I later asked Erv why he hadn't come upstairs to check on me, knowing I was upset about something. He replied: *"Bruh, ain't nobody tryin' to hear or see you! Up there listenin' to sh*t like Mary J. Blige – 'Not Gon' Cry'. All the while, you probably makin' that ugly a** cry face!? Nah bruh (shaking his head), I'm good on that."* Even though I had never played any such music, I couldn't do anything but laugh.

Despite Jason being my younger brother, he was always very protective of me. I remember we were once at a shoe store in the mall, when suddenly, Erv came up and put his arm around me, as if we were dating. I instantly said: *"What are you doing!?"* He whispered back: *"Shut up! Them thugs over there starin' and talkin' 'bout you. And I don't want either one of them approachin' you!"* – smh, lol. In his defense, when I glanced over at the guys he was referring to, I was kind of glad Erv did what he did.

Speaking of shoes, that was one thing Erv and I had in common – we LOVED retro Jordan's. Each of us had our own little collection. Although Erv probably bought the majority of his own, there were several occasions in which I got tricked into buying them for him – coincidently, the most expensive pairs. (In hindsight and knowing Erv, this was probably no coincidence at all.)

Since I made more money than him (and to tell the truth, because he was spoiled), I'd often offer to help pay for his Jordan's. For example, I'd agree to put his shoes on my credit card provided he'd give me half the money back when he received his next paycheck. He'd always say: *"Ok, cool. I got you."* He NEVER had me.

Alternatively, I'd buy him a pair earlier in the year, under the pretense that the shoes would serve as his birthday or Christmas gift. He'd always agree: *"Ok, cool."* But I'd ALWAYS end up buying him something else (usually another pair of shoes) on his birthday or for Christmas.

In addition to nice shoes, Jason and I also loved nice clothes and nice cars. Both of us shopped quite often, especially Jason. He hated repeating outfits on the weekends. He always wanted to look "fresh" when he went out, so he'd at least purchase or wear a new shirt if he had plans to hit the town. Even though I rarely went out on the weekends, I felt the same way about my outfits. Therefore, I was constantly buying new tops, dresses, and shoes.

Jason and I were fortunate enough to have had our own cars since we were in our teens. But it wasn't until we were in Atlanta that we each got our "dream car." Jason got a newer model Chevy Camaro, and it was beautiful! It was dark red with two grey race stripes down the middle. Jason absolutely loved that car. He took pride in it and kept it super clean. I can hardly remember a time when the Camaro was dirty.

On my 30th birthday, I decided to treat myself to a brand-new BMW 4-series coupe. It was black with red leather interior and fully loaded. It had *all* the bells and whistles! I fell in love with it the moment I saw it at the dealership.

When the deal was done, I remember not only feeling excited, but also extremely thankful, blessed, and accomplished. (Not many single people can say by age 30 they received a doctorate degree, earned a 6-figure salary, purchased a home, and owned two cars – with no cosigner on any of the three purchases – but I could.)

Erv and I also loved to eat, especially pizza. It was our favorite food. We'd have it at least once a week. We'd also go out to eat quite often. This was always comical, because whenever the waiter or waitress would give Erv the ticket, he'd always slide it over to me saying: *"It's on me next time."* It was NEVER on him.

In addition, going out to eat with him when he first graduated culinary school was *always* an experience. First of all, he always wore a chef coat. To me, that was funny in and of itself. I remember asking: *"Why are you wearing a chef coat!?"* His response: *"Because we're going out to eat. And I'ma chef. Duh!"*

I also remember going to brunch once with him and some friends: Jason had ordered a steak as part of his meal. When the waitress brought it out, he touched it with a single finger and said to her in an uppity chef-like tone: *"This is overdone. Can you send it back?"* Everyone at the table laughed when the waitress walked away. I remember thinking: *"What the hell!? Who does he think he is!?"*

Erv and I had another similar interest: tattoos. We got our first couple tattoos together at Kreations Tattoo and Body Piercing in Huntsville, owned by husband and wife, Adam and Kristi Fellhoelter. In fact, Kristi and Adam did all our tattoo work, with the exception of one tattoo Erv had done at a local shop in Atlanta. Erv eventually became obsessed with getting tattoos and left me in the dust. I stopped counting once he got to ten, considering I was still on tattoo number two.

- **The Four of Us**

In addition to our sibling bond growing as we got older, the relationship Jason and I had with our parents also grew. He and I had always been family oriented, but we found ourselves spending more time together as a family once Jason and I became adults.

To celebrate our graduations in 2010, the four of us decided to go on a cruise. We enjoyed the trip so much that we made it a tradition and began going on one every summer. The cruise ship had something for all of us to do or enjoy, both individually and collectively: shows, gambling, swimming pools, a nightclub, and all the food we could eat, including a 24-hour pizzeria! (*If you've never been on a cruise, you really should consider it. It's like several vacations in one. You won't regret it. I promise!*)

In addition to our annual cruises, the four of us would also take random trips, for instance, to the beach or to the casino. Other times we'd simply hang out, either in Atlanta or in Huntsville. And just like Jason and I, the four of us would watch TV, talk, and laugh – usually at our in-house comedian, Erv. Additionally, we'd often order pizza (we all loved pizza, lol) or go out to eat or to a movie. In short, we just loved each other's company.

Also important to note, as a family we were huge Dallas Cowboys football fans. Since my dad was always a big fan of the Cowboys, they were the only team Jason and I heard about growing up. Unfortunately, between school and work obligations, the four of us were never able to coordinate our schedules to attend a game.

But when we saw the 2017 roster, we noticed they would be playing the Atlanta Falcons in November – in Atlanta. The game was on a Sunday that everyone happened to have off from work. The four of us were so excited about the chance to FINALLY attend a Cowboys game.

In addition to me spoiling Jason with shoes and free meals, my parents also spoiled him – a lot – starting from childhood. For example, growing up my dad never made Jason responsible for cutting the grass. Nonetheless, when I moved into my house, my parents bought me a new lawnmower under the assumption Jason would begin cutting the grass once he moved in. They assumed wrong.

I remember the grass getting high and saying*: "Erv, when are you gonna put the lawnmower together and cut the grass? It's getting high, and I'm not tryin' to be fined by the HOA."** He responded: "Girl, I ain't cuttin' no grass! Who I look like!? You better put that thing together yo self and get to mowin'! Or call somebody to come cut that sh*t. 'Cause I ain't cuttin' no grass bruh." – lol.

I couldn't even be mad at Erv. My parents had never made him cut their grass, so why would he cut ours? As a result, I ended up

---

* Home Owners Association.

hiring someone to maintain our lawn. My parents also returned the lawnmower and got their money back.

My parents (and I) would also spoil Jason in other ways, particularly by giving him money from time to time. He'd always jokingly respond: *"Thanks for donating to the poor," or, "God bless you."* In the rare instance in which they'd give us both money, he'd ask them: *"What y'all givin' her money for!? I'm the one that's poor!"* Half the time, I'd end up giving the money they gave me to him, or at the very least, splitting it with him.

I also learned I wasn't the only victim of Jason's *"I got you"* promise. He did my mom the same way with a credit card they shared. The original plan was for Jason to use the card for emergencies only, and she would take care of the bill.

However, Jason pretty much used the card for any- and everything. When she'd call him about a high bill (which was often), I'd hear him saying something along the lines of: *"My bad Sarah! But I got you. I'll start making payments to help get the balance down."*

Jason never made one payment. But in his defense, I will say my mom never asked him to help with the payments, nor did she ever take him up on his offer and make him pay. She just wanted him to "do better." He never did any better.

Career Paths and Interactions

- **The Pharmacist**

I worked for the same company the entire length of my pharmacy career. I started out as a pharmacy technician while in college; became an intern upon entering pharmacy school; and ultimately became a registered pharmacist after completing the Doctor of Pharmacy program and passing my licensure exams in 2010.

When I began practicing in Huntsville, I held a staff pharmacist position. This was also the title I carried upon transferring my pharmacy position to Atlanta. I worked in the store I was transferred to for about six months before being placed in a different store. After working at the second store for about a year and a half, I returned to my original store. Soon after returning, however, I was promoted from staff pharmacist to pharmacy manager.

The pharmacy manager role came with A LOT of responsibility. I still had to ensure my routine pharmacist roles and responsibilities were taken care of during each of my shifts. This included but was not limited to overseeing the general operation of the pharmacy; technician scheduling; verifying accuracy and safety of filled medications; communicating with healthcare providers; administering immunizations; and counseling patients on prescription and over-the-counter medications.

In addition to these and other tasks, I had manager-specific duties including, but not limited to being held ultimately accountable for *all* pharmacy operations at my store; technician staffing; staff pharmacist and technician reviews; completing routine regulatory reviews; creating monthly pharmacy action plans; handling customer concerns and complaints; and attending district meetings.

Despite the additional workload, I embraced the pharmacy manager role. I've never been one to back down from a challenge, and this was no different. Plus, still being relatively new to the district and only age 30 at the time, I was humbled that my manager thought enough of me and my work ethic to select me for the promotion. After all, I never applied for, or actively sought, the pharmacy manager position. It was given to me.

While practicing in Huntsville and at the second store in Atlanta, Jason would come visit me from time to time and was always protective when it came to hostile customers. I vividly remember an incident that occurred in Huntsville: The store I worked at was notorious for having customers attempt to buy pseudoephedrine products from behind the pharmacy counter for illegitimate purposes.[*]

One day, Jason happened to be visiting and witnessed me refuse to sell pseudoephedrine to a customer, whom I suspected was not purchasing the medication for a legitimate reason. Although I didn't hear him, the customer walked by Jason and said: *"You f***ing cunt!"* Immediately after, I saw and heard Erv turn around and reply: *"What the f*** you say 'bout my sister!?"* That guy literally took off running out of the store.

After the customer took off, I asked Erv what was said to make him snap like that in response. When he told me what the guy called me, I replied: *"Aww Erv, don't worry about that. Those meth-heads get mad at me all the time. I don't care."* Erv responded: *"Well, I do! I ain't gon' let nobody disrespect you like that in my presence. You work here, not me. [So,] I ain't got nothin' to lose!"*

A similar incident occurred at my second store in Atlanta, in which I refused to fill a prescription for a patient. However, since the guy didn't blatantly disrespect me (he was just very hostile), Erv did

---

[*] Pseudoephedrine is one of the active ingredients used to make the street drug, methamphetamine or "meth."

not confront him. Instead he sat in the waiting area until the customer left the store. I assume, just in case the guy "got out of line."

Soon after Erv left the pharmacy, he came right back, saying the guy was still at the store, standing outside in the parking lot. He then said: *"He might try to bring his crazy a** back in here (shaking his head). I ain't leavin' bruh."* And Erv literally stayed in the pharmacy waiting area until the customer left the property.

When I returned to my original store, Jason began to visit more often. His job at the time was nearby, as well as the Chevy dealership where he had his Camaro serviced. I never knew in advance that he'd be stopping by. Instead, he would just pop up at the consultation window of the pharmacy, often obnoxiously yelling something like: *"Excuse me! Excuse me! Can I get a consultation!? Excuse me!"* – lol.

Half the time he'd change his voice, so I wouldn't know it was him until I looked up, and he'd be there at the window smiling from ear to ear. Coincidentally, it seemed like he'd always show up on my worst or busiest days – the days when I could use a laugh or needed to smile. And although he'd only stay a few minutes, I always felt so much better after seeing him.

In addition to Erv visiting more frequently, we'd also talk on the phone at some point during almost each of my shifts, usually around 3 p.m. through the week, when Jason got off from work. I'd call him most of the time, but if he didn't answer I could always count on him to quickly return my call. He called the pharmacy so frequently that the technicians eventually recognized his number on the caller ID. Anytime the phone read "WIRELESS CALLER" with a

256- phone number, the technicians would say: *"Ebony, that's Jason calling!"*

The staff at every store I've worked at grew to know and love Jason. It was as if he were an "honorary employee." Once settled in Atlanta, I began hosting my team's annual Christmas party at our house. Jason would always attend and be the life of the party. Often, by the end of the night he'd turn my "team-building activity" into a full-blown party with music, alcohol, and a competitive game of beer pong.

Whenever my friends from work and I would plan an outing, such as meeting for brunch, Jason would often go with us, and per usual, I'd end up paying for both of us. Even when I'd make it clear beforehand that we were "going Dutch," so he'd be responsible for his own bill, I'd *still* end up paying.

Before leaving home, he'd always agree to pay for his food. Then later, when the waiter or waitress would ask if we all needed separate checks, he'd point to me and say: *"Oh, nah. We're together."* And when the person would hand him the ticket, he'd slide it over to me, saying his infamous line: *"It's on me next time."* Needless to say, it was never on him.

- **The Chef**

Jason graduated from Le Cordon Bleu College of Culinary Arts Atlanta in 2010. Unlike most new chefs, he chose to not go into the restaurant business. Instead he opted to join the corporate culinary work force, initially working for companies such as Sodexo and Aramark.

As a Sodexo employee, he prepared food for a couple different corporations in the Atlanta area. He worked for Sodexo as a line cook for a little over three years before taking a chef position with Sage Dining Services at Wesleyan (Private) School in Peachtree Corners.

While working full-time for Sodexo, Jason also worked part-time (seasonally) for Aramark. The Aramark position was affiliated with Turner Field, former home of the Atlanta Braves baseball team. Jason worked for Aramark for a little over 5 years, starting as a line cook at the field's 755 Club and working his way up to a chef supervisor position.[*]

Jason thrived as a chef at Wesleyan. This was the first position in which his talent and creativity as a chef were fully displayed. Since the school was privately owned, their culinary program focused on providing quality and nutritious meals for the students, faculty, and staff. Jason would often post pictures of the food he prepared on his social media accounts. One day I said to him: *"Damn, those kids eat way better than we did growin' up."* He jokingly replied: *"Hell, those kids eat better than we do now!"*

In addition to his culinary skills being on display, Jason's personality also shined bright at the private school. Not only did he get along well with his colleagues, but he also made an impression on the students, faculty, and staff. He made it a point to remember the names of any- and everyone who knew his, often giving the kids nicknames. He loved working at the school and often had a story to share about his interactions. He'd end almost every story saying: *"I'm telling you Eb…they love me at that school, especially them kids."*

---

[*] 755 Club was a private restaurant located on the Turner Field grounds.

Jason worked for the school for a little over a year before accepting a full-time position at Turner Field with their new food service provider, Delaware North. On his last day at the school, Jason described how, not only the students, but also members of the faculty and staff, lined up to hug him and say their goodbyes, many of them giving cards, flowers, or gifts. He said a lot of the younger students even cried, making his own eyes water.

I was shocked when I came home from work and saw everything he received. There were flowers covering every bit of counter space we had. There was also a stack of cards filled with kind words, many of which also had money or a gift card inside. He also received quite a few nice gifts – for example, a Dallas Cowboys apron with matching chef hat and a Louisville Slugger baseball bat, which some of the students had signed.

The 5th grade class went so far as to make a 7-foot banner full of well-wishes and their signatures. Later, some of the kids attended Braves games and visited Jason at his restaurant, introducing him to their parents. Jason was definitely right. They loved him at that school.

At Delaware North (Turner Field), Jason was promoted to chef de partie of The Braves Chop House restaurant.[*] As part of his training, Delaware North sent him and a few of his colleagues to Roanoke, Virginia for several weeks. Jason enjoyed himself while working in Virginia, often posting his experiences on social media. In fact, he had grown so fond of the people he was working and living

---

[*] A chef de partie oversees a particular area of production in a restaurant. In large kitchens, each chef de partie might have several cooks or assistants. (Wikipedia)

with that, for a brief moment, he contemplated transferring his position to Roanoke.

Even though the chef de partie position was a promotion, it still wasn't the position Jason had hoped for. He longed to be in upper-level culinary management. Although he was still young (age 29), he was very ambitious and confident that he could succeed if given the opportunity to prove himself. Therefore, he continued applying for management positions while working for Delaware North.

Toward the end of 2016, Jason's prayers were answered. He had applied for and was offered a position with Sodexo as a food service manager (FSM) for the Atlanta Public Schools System, or APS, starting the first week in January. The supervisor had been impressed with Jason's work at the private school and was looking forward to having him assist with improving the APS' culinary program.

Jason was ecstatic. After ending the call with the supervisor, I remember him saying: *"Finally! Finally! Thank you, God! Thank you!"* In addition to Jason having the kind of title he desired, the position also came with a pay increase. In fact, he'd be making more money as an FSM than he had ever made with any of his previous two-job combinations. And since the position was affiliated with APS, he no longer had to worry about working nights, weekends, or holidays. Lastly, the position was salaried, so he'd also be paid during summer breaks – even though he wouldn't be in the office full-time.

Although everything seemed great about the position, there was one downside (well, in Jason's opinion): the dress code. Although he would be visiting different school kitchens, ultimately the FSM position was an office job. This meant, he had to swap his chef coat and pants for business casual attire, and even worse – his kitchen shoes for "church shoes."

I laugh when I think back on this: The first week of the job, Jason followed suit with the dress code. He wore button-up shirts (tucked in), slacks, and casual dress shoes. I remember him complaining literally every day about how he looked and how uncomfortable he felt. He'd shake his head saying: *"This look just ain't me…I be feeling so uncomfortable in this sh*t."*

The second week, Erv kept the slacks and shoes but wore his shirt untucked. Getting away with that small change, the following week he continued wearing the shoes but stopped wearing slacks and started wearing black chef pants instead, claiming they were more comfortable. By week four, I noticed he had started incorporating polo-style shirts and wearing Jordan's – but only pairs that were solid black.

After that first month, Erv's original dress code was completely out the window. He had started color coordinating his shirts with his different Jordan's. When I asked him about the wardrobe change, he said: *"Man, I had to let that sh*t go. I went wit' it at first, 'cause I was the new kid on the block. But I'm in there now! [And] when no one said anything about my polos and them black J's, it was a wrap bruh!"*

Jason loved his new job and everything about it. He really liked the fact that his time was divided between being at the office and visiting schools. So, every day was a different experience. Plus, the position allowed him to travel out of state, all expenses paid, for special programs and trainings. Had it not been for the job, he probably would've never visited such places.

Lastly, and probably what Erv liked most about the position, was that he could save money each pay period without having to sacrifice the things he loved: shopping for clothes, buying shoes, and going out on the weekends.

In addition to having a culinary management position, Jason was also interested in becoming a private caterer. He and a friend had catered an event once in the past, and he loved it. Not to mention, the pay was great.

In April of 2017, Jason got his first opportunity to complete a large-scale catering job by himself. Jason clients were a couple who were hosting a party to celebrate their wedding anniversary. They chartered a riverboat and held the event on Lake Lanier Islands (Georgia). I had to work that weekend, so my mom came in town to help him with some of the leg work.

The catering ended up being a huge success. Everything turned out great. Jason was so proud of the food he had prepared, all of which he posted on his social media accounts. The clients were pleased with his work as well, and many of the guests took his contact information for future events. When Erv made it home that night, my mom and I could see the sense of accomplishment on his face.

Although Jason loved to cook and cater, he never abandoned his first love or passion: music. He created numerous tracks and several mixtapes over the span of at least 10 years, from his different "home studios," using *J. Erv* as his stage name.* And no, he wasn't just a "wanna be rapper." In fact, although rap/hip-hop was his genre

---

* "Tracks" and "mixtapes" refer to songs and unofficial albums, respectively.

of choice, he never considered himself a rapper. Instead, he preferred the term "lyricist."

In my opinion, lyricist was a more accurate label for Erv, because he had unbelievable bars and punchlines.[*] He could freestyle with ease, and his style and delivery on tracks was super versatile.[†] In addition, he knew how to mix and master music. He dabbled in beat production. And believe it or not, he could sing a little bit as well. All of which he did with no formal training, just pure talent. A true musician. And I was his biggest cheerleader AND critic if need be. So, I'm not just saying all this because he's my brother.

Erv also recorded several songs with Reu and Matt (stage names: *J. Reu* and *Aérostotle*, respectively), as one-third of their group, *Redstone,* or as a feature on their solo projects. Although they would usually record at Erv's home studios, they'd often record at professional studios as well. All three of them were talented in their own rights, and the music they created collectively was just as good as their individual projects.

Social Interactions

Jason and I were complete social opposites. I've always been a homebody – only going out on a rare occasion, especially if the outing

---

[*] "Bars and punchlines" refer to lyrical content or phrases (bars) that are intelligent, clever, or witty...having a similar impact or effect on the listener as a comedic punchline has on an audience or viewer.

[†] To "freestyle" is the ability to improvise and recite rhymes or lyrics with no prior preparation or knowledge of the subject matter.

was associated with the nightlife. I pretty much only cared to go to concerts (assuming Chris Brown or Kirk Franklin was on the ticket), comedy shows, movies, out to eat with friends, etc.

Jason, on the other hand, was a social butterfly who never met a stranger. He loved to have a good time, go out, party, and experience the nightlife. Erv was the epitome of someone who ate, drank, and was merry. In fact, he was the self-proclaimed "Turn-up King!" And that's exactly what he did – often.

Jason loved going out on the weekends, especially to nightclubs. Although he would sometimes go with Reu and Matt or his other close friend, A.J., often times he'd go by himself – on his *"solo dolo"* as he would say. And although he seldom drank at home, he was definitely a social drinker. His favorite drink was a top shelf long island iced tea.

Erv not only loved the club atmosphere, but also to dance. He'd often describe getting behind a girl and *"working his magic."* I, on the other hand, pretty much gave up the nightclub scene after college. And even when I did go to the club, I hardly ever danced. I'd usually just be a fly on the wall, plus or minus a drink in my hand – usually minus.

On the contrary, I did dance at home – a lot. Especially, when Jason and I would be in the kitchen cooking together. It was nothing for me to start dancing or twerking. Mind you, I'm not the best at either. (Jason definitely had the most rhythm between the two of us.)

It was nothing for Erv to say in these instances: *"Will you cut that sh*t out!? [You] know yo a** can't dance,"* or, *"So you wanna dance at the house, but won't go to the club? And hell, even if ya did go, you'd probably just be standing there, with the same cup in ya* *hand all night."* (He knew me so well.) And if I decided to twerk, he'd often just put his hand up and say: *"Eww. Gross."*

Even though Jason didn't make a large amount of money as a chef, he still made it a point to party, to travel, and to just live his life and have fun while doing it. I remember him once saying: *"Eb, if I was a pharmacist and made the kinda money you do! Giiirl! I'd be in the club, getting sections, buying bottles. You wouldn't be able to tell me nothin'! Pour up! Drinks on me!"* – lol.

Me being the older, more responsible one, I would always encourage him to save more. I'd say things like: *"Erv, you went to Mardi Gras last year. You don't have to go again this year,"* or, *"You just went out last weekend. You ain't gotta go out this weekend. Why don't you just chill at home?"* Until one day, he replied: *"Eb, I'm not like you. All you do is work. It's almost like you're livin', just to f***in' work! But me? Eb, the only reason why I work, is so I can live."*

And Erv was right. All I did was work. Even when I wasn't physically at the pharmacy, I might as well have been, as I was often mentally there. On my "off" days, I'd still find myself thinking about work, checking emails, completing online trainings, or sending text messages to my team. Plus, I spent so much time *at* work, that when I *was* scheduled to be off, I was often too tired to do anything social – even if I wanted to.

In hindsight, it's almost crazy to think that as a pharmacist, I made three to four times Jason's salary for most of his career as a chef. Yet, he had traveled to more places and experienced more social activities and events than I had. And although, I didn't cut back on my hours or become much more social after his remark, it was definitely an eye-opener. Because like he also once said: *"What's the point of makin' all that money, if you're not gonna enjoy it? Or even worse, if you're too tired to enjoy it?"*

Despite the difference in my and Jason's social affairs, one thing we both loved to do was entertain guests by hosting parties and events at our house. In addition to hosting my team's annual Christmas Party, Erv and I would often host super bowl parties and random get-togethers or cookouts for our friends and coworkers.

Erv and I would always provide and prepare all the food ourselves. Additionally, since Erv was a social drinker, he always made sure we had plenty of alcohol. Lastly, he always made sure his beer pong table was set up. And by the end of the night, he always managed to find someone to play with.

One of the biggest and nicest parties we hosted was in celebration of Erv's "Dirty 30" (and my 32nd) birthday in 2016. Erv and I prepared more food than we ever had, as our guest list was longer than it had ever been. I even went so far as to hire a party hostess to assist during the event, so Erv and I could truly enjoy ourselves – not having to worry about greeting people at the door, restocking the food and drinks, or cleaning up after the event.

The event ended up being a huge success and lasted until the wee hours of the next morning. The turn-out was GREAT. Not only did most of our coworkers and local friends attend, but we also had friends come from out of town, some of whom we hadn't seen in years. Also, everyone loved the food. Some people even took things to-go, as there was plenty to go around.

Erv and I truly enjoyed ourselves during that party. In fact, I drank more alcohol that night, than I probably had the entire year. I remember Erv – being the protective brother that he was – approaching me and asking: *"How many drinks you done had?"*

I responded by shrugging my shoulders and saying: *"I don't know, a few?"* He replied: *"Yeah. You're done,"* and proceeded to take my cup out of my hand. I responded: *"What you doin'!?"* He said: *"You heard me! You're done. No more drinks for you. [You] know yo a** is a lightweight drinker."* I couldn't do anything but laugh. I was also done drinking for the night.

Dating and Relationships

Growing up and even into adulthood, Jason and I didn't have many serious romantic relationships – maybe two or three each by the time we settled in Atlanta. Once in Atlanta, each of us only had one true relationship during the time in which we lived together, neither of which ultimately lasted.

Additionally, neither of us had any children by this time. However, when our mom retired from her job, she would always inquire about our plans for marriage and starting a family. Obviously, she was looking forward to becoming a grandparent.

Jason would often respond to her inquiry by saying: *"Now Sarah, if you want some grandkids, I can get you some grandkids! Now, you may not have a daughter-in-law. But I can get you a baby – if that's all you want."* While laughing, my mom would always exclaim: *"No! No! No! I want a daughter-in-law first!"*

Jason and I were always protective about the people the other sibling chose to date. And although we may not have taken heed to each other's concerns about a person (or at least not initially), we still valued each other's opinion. Also, the other sibling's thoughts and opinions carried a lot of weight. Our bond was so tight, and our family was so close-knit that we ultimately knew, if the other sibling (or our parents) didn't care for the person, chances are the relationship wouldn't work out in the long run.

In terms of dating, I was the more protective sibling, hands down. Going as far back as high school, if Jason brought a girl (or later a woman) around that I didn't care for or got a negative vibe from, I let him know *immediately* – whether solicited or not. Nonetheless, I never wanted to hurt the person's (or more importantly, Jason's) feelings, so I'd always be cordial in their presence. But that was the best I could do.

If I didn't like you for my brother, then I wasn't going to pretend to like you or be supportive of the relationship (or a potential relationship). This is not to say that Jason didn't bring around nice girls, because he did. He definitely had standards. But unfortunately for most of those girls – so did I.

When it came to the men I dated, Jason didn't necessarily give unsolicited advice or opinions. However, if I sought his opinion or complained to him about a guy, he held absolutely nothing back and had no regard for my feelings. He gave me his unfiltered thoughts or perspective, not only as my brother and best friend, but also (and probably more importantly) – as a man.

Although I didn't always take heed to Erv's advice, it *definitely* remained in the back of my mind. And just like I was usually right about the girls or women he dated, more often than not, he was right about my guys.

Yet and still, Jason and I were both optimistic about eventually finding "the one" to settle down with, get married to, and have kids with. We always said we'd raise our children to not only be best friends with their siblings (like the two of us), but also best friends with their cousins, instilling the value of family in them as our parents had with us.

Jason and I would also laugh and talk about the traditions we'd start with the new generation – for example, sending them to their grandparents' house in Huntsville once a month or during summer breaks. In short, we were looking forward to the next chapter in our lives.

Chapter 5: The Gym

"God created it. Jesus died for it.
The Spirit lives in it. I'd better take care of it."
– Pastor Rick Warren

One thing Jason and I both had in common for most of our childhood was obesity. I ended up losing much of my excess weight during puberty and through specific dietary changes.[*] Nevertheless, keeping the weight off has always been a struggle. Jason remained overweight throughout his high school years and on into college. He eventually went on to have gastric bypass surgery and lost well over 100 pounds.

After surgery, Jason began living a healthier lifestyle. This is also when he developed an interest in cooking, and subsequently, entertained the idea of becoming a chef. Nonetheless, like myself, keeping his weight in check was a battle he constantly had to fight.

Physical fitness became a large part of our lives in Atlanta. Upon my return to the city, I joined a nearby private fitness studio, Trendsetter Training, owned by certified personal trainer, Caleb Jones.[†] Caleb was young, athletic, and full of energy. I loved his vibe and his passion for physical fitness.

---

[*] In 1999, I excluded beef and pork from my diet and all beverages other than water. Although I now occasionally have other beverages, I have not consumed beef or pork since.

[†] Names (Trendsetter, Caleb) have been changed.

In addition, I liked what his facility had to offer. Although it was an intimate space, Caleb had the latest machines and equipment, some of which, I had never been exposed to before. He also led a unique class, *Burn 1000*, a few times a week that clients could take in addition to personal training. With the opportunity to experience such new physical activities, I was excited about the possibilities that lied ahead in my fitness journey.

Soon after joining the gym, I not only realized how close Caleb (or C, as most people called him) was to his clients, but also, how close his clients were to one another. It was as if they were one big "Trendsetter family," and I was glad to now be a part of it. I enjoyed my initial experience at the gym so much that I soon talked Erv into visiting with me.

The energy at Trendsetter was contagious. As a result, Erv ended up joining the gym as well. Just like me, he liked C's vibe and respected his passion for fitness. Additionally, since they both had a football background, he liked and appreciated C's training style. In fact, Erv spent so much time at the gym that he eventually started looking up to C, almost like a big brother.

With Caleb only having a few male clients at the time, he welcomed Jason's masculine energy and quickly grew fond of him as well. On more than one occasion, Erv joked: *"Eb, that dude wishes I was his brother, man. I know he do! You see how much he like having me around."*

Before long, everyone knew the two of us. I can't even count the number of times we were asked if we were twins when we worked out together. Even when we weren't together, clients would ask me: *"Hey, do you have a brother?"* Or they'd ask Erv: *"Do you have a sister that works out here?"* It always tickled me because people have mentioned how much the two of us looked alike, but I never thought our resemblance was *that* close.

Under Caleb's guidance, Erv and I got in the best shape of our lives! Not just aesthetically, but also in terms of our athletic performance and conditioning. We were doing physical activities that we never would've committed to on our own, the best example being distance running.

Jason and I started doing 5-mile runs around Stone Mountain Park and participating in different types of races throughout the city: 5Ks, 10Ks, obstacle courses, etc. Long story short, we were running! And Erv thrived at it. In fact, he was one of the few clients with race times comparable to Caleb's. After running a close race with Caleb, he'd say: *"C will never admit it, but I be keeping him on his toes at these races!"*

A couple years later, Caleb merged his business with a new and upcoming public fitness center: The Fitness Center of Lilburn (TFC). This is when and where Erv and I truly became workout buddies. With TFC being open every day, he and I worked out together several times a week – whether taking part in one of C's classes or doing our own thing together.

Before long, both members and staff at TFC knew our faces (and asked if we were twins) just like at Trendsetter. Additionally, because TFC was a new and independent venture, with very few members initially (the majority of whom came from C's gym), it still had that private and "family" feel that had originally attracted us to Trendsetter.

Also worth mentioning, TFC, although open to the public, was affiliated with New Mercies Christian Church. They actually shared the same parking lot. During the development stages of TFC, I had the pleasure of meeting the church's pastor, Jesse Curney, III.

I loved Pastor Curney's spirit and later introduced him to Jason. He quickly became fond of both of us, stopping to speak anytime he'd see either of us in the gym. Eventually, my mom (who had joined TFC to utilize when she visited) was able to meet Pastor Curney as well.

Over time our "TFC family" grew. However, more people knew and recognized Jason because he would often go to the gym during peak (afternoon) hours. And unlike mine, his work schedule allowed him to participate in more of C's classes. Plus, Erv was more outgoing and had that "never met a stranger" personality. You could often hear him motivating and pushing clients during Caleb's classes almost as much (if not more) than C. If you didn't know any better, you'd think C had an assistant trainer.

As for Erv and I, we truly became each other's gym motivation at TFC. We held each other accountable and pushed each other to challenge our limits and strength. We were *swolemates*.[*] Erv focused on the barbell bench press, to work and build his chest, while, I focused on the squat rack, to work and build my legs and glutes.

Eventually, Jason and I both became super strong on our respective machines, so much so, that our strength and muscle growth became a source of pride for both of us. Being a female, I was extremely proud. My strength easily surpassed the other females at

---

[*] A "swolemate" is a trendy name for a gym buddy or workout partner.

TFC, and truth be told, some of the men as well. I can hear Erv now: *"Wit' yo buff a**!"* – lol.

Erv had a very competitive attitude in the gym – especially when it came to C's other clients, whether male or female and regardless of the activity. I, on the other hand, didn't care to compete. I just focused on myself. In fact, Caleb used to say the one thing I lacked in my athleticism was that *"competitive edge"* or the *"dog"* in me as he would describe it. But he was wrong. I had that *"dog"* in me. But it only came out when I was up against Erv. You know, sibling rivalry.

My competitive side quickly surfaced whenever C paired Erv and I to run sprints on the track. I competed with him not only because we were siblings, but also because he talked sooo much trash – from start to finish. And what made it even more annoying (and funny) was *how* he'd talk to me.

We'd be at the start line, and he'd whisper: *"You know you not gon' beat me."* Then, if he was ahead while we were running, he'd be yelling: *"Catch up lil' girl! Catch up!"* or, *"You can't beat me! You can't beat me girl!"* And if he won, he'd say something like: *"Eb, I don't know how many times I gotta tell yo a**, you can't beat me dawg!"* followed by a pat on the shoulder or some other insulting gesture.

Erv taunted me like that every single time we raced. So, I always tried my hardest to beat him – just to shut him up. Now, to be honest, Erv would beat me most of the time. But every now and then, I'd get a win on him. And those would be my proudest moments in the gym, hands down.

Chapter 6: The Family Pet

"The world would be a nicer place if everyone had the
ability to love as unconditionally as a dog."
– M.K. Clinton

Mercer was my first choice for pharmacy school because of its location in Atlanta, Rob's hometown. Rob and I had been college sweethearts. He had transferred to Stillman from a college in Atlanta to play football. As a result, he ended up spending an additional semester at Stillman after I graduated. However, I knew that upon completion of his courses, he would be moving back home to Atlanta for good.

Unfortunately, my relationship with Rob ended during my first semester of pharmacy school. Considering I didn't have any other friends or family in the Atlanta area at the time, I found myself both alone and lonely. It wasn't long before I became depressed. In addition, with the new-found stress of pharmacy school, I was often anxious and frequently experiencing panic attacks. The panic attacks were difficult to manage in and of themselves, and the combination of both the depression and anxiety was almost crippling.

Per my mom's suggestion, I eventually sought medical attention, scheduling an appointment with Mercer's on-campus psychiatrist. As a result, I was diagnosed with clinical depression and generalized anxiety disorder. I was prescribed two medications: Lexapro (an anti-depressant) and Xanax (an anxiolytic).

I ended up only using the Xanax for about two weeks. I could only take it at night, because it made me so sleepy that I couldn't tolerate it during the day, when I needed it most. And although it was nice to get a good night's rest, I decided not to continue taking the medication since it wasn't helping resolve my primary issue: the anxiety and subsequent panic attacks.

I stayed on the Lexapro for about six months before deciding to discontinue it as well. The potential side effects of the drug didn't sit well with me. And more importantly, I wasn't convinced that it was truly helping my depression (as I didn't notice a major difference in my mood). Ultimately, I figured I would have to find non-medicinal ways to manage my anxiety and depression.

I eventually decided I wanted to get a puppy, against the recommendation of my parents not to do so. I explained that I felt having a puppy would help solve one of the major causes of my depression: being lonely. My parents didn't necessarily disagree with my reasoning. They just felt that owning a pet, especially during pharmacy school, could potentially be overwhelming. Thus, contributing to my anxiety.

Plus, my parents reasoned that Jason and I didn't have any pets growing up. Therefore, I had no idea what owning a pet dog truly entailed. Nonetheless, I was determined to become a dog owner.

After doing some brief research on the different dog breeds and crossbreeds, I decided to get a puggle – a cross between a pug and a beagle. My primary reason for choosing a puggle was simply because I thought they were so cute! With my decision made, I searched for a breeder and found one in Tennessee.

Soon after, I was the proud owner of a 6-week old female puggle. Because I had gotten her to help with my depression, coming up with her name was easy: Lexi. I essentially ditched the drug, Lexapro, for my dog, Lexi.

Initially, my parents were right. Having Lexi proved to be the biggest mistake of my life! I can laugh about it now, but there was nothing funny about it back then. To start, although I don't recall Lexi making a sound on the trip from Tennessee back to my parent's house, I can vividly remember her crying the entire three and a half hours from Huntsville to Atlanta the following day.

If that weren't bad enough, in the middle of every night Lexi would wake up and cry, just like a newborn baby. And the only way I knew to quiet her, was to place her on my chest until she fell back asleep.

Under normal circumstances, this may have been a little more tolerable. But for me that wasn't the case. I was already sleep deprived from the excessive studying I had to do. So, the routine of waking up during the night to cater to Lexi got old quickly. As a result, I had to break her crying habit by refusing to get up when she cried. After several restless nights, Lexi finally began to sleep through the night. Praise God!

Eventually, however, Lexi became a much-loved part of our family, especially my parents. During the time when I had been practicing pharmacy in Huntsville, my dad had gotten laid off from his job. Since that rendered him free during the day, he would help me out with Lexi when I had to work my 13-hour shifts. It was during that time that he became very fond of Lexi.

Similarly, when my mom retired from her job in 2013, she decided that her and my dad would keep Lexi in Huntsville full-time. Although I had moved back to Atlanta by that time, I was still working long shifts at the pharmacy, so Lexi being at home with my parents was for the best. I think Jason was the most excited because he no longer was responsible for letting her out of her crate when I had to work.

Jason was easily the least fond of Lexi, but she was crazy about him. She loved being up under him in our den. And any chance she got, she would sneak into the basement – whether Jason was down there or not. Often times, she'd be looking for leftover food in his room, but I'd like to think sometimes she was just looking for him.

Normally, Lexi's presence in the basement would go undetected if Jason wasn't there. But every now and then, despite her being fully housetrained, she'd leave behind a little "surprise" for Jason when he returned. I'm pretty sure this was the main reason he didn't want her in his space. Nonetheless, Lexi eventually grew on Jason as well, and he learned to love her just as much as the rest of us.

All four of us spoiled Lexi – not only with attention, but also with food and treats. As a result, Lexi became overweight. Lexi also suffered from terrible allergies and was placed on long-term steroid therapy. This hindered any potential weight loss efforts, and eventually led to Lexi developing diabetes and requiring insulin injections. To make matters worse, as a complication of the diabetes, my mom later informed me that Lexi had begun losing her sight as well.

With everything going on with Lexi's health, I told my mom I wanted to see her. So, she and Lexi made a trip to Atlanta and stayed with me and Jason for about two weeks. It hurt my heart that upon "seeing" me, Lexi didn't realize who I was until she was close enough to smell me. I spent as much time as I could loving on Lexi those two weeks, and I'm glad I did. That was my last time seeing her.

Soon after she and my mom returned to Huntsville, Lexi got acutely sick. And a few days later, on October 16, 2015, Lexi had to be put down. Everyone took it hard, even Erv. Lexi was a part of our family – a special part. When it came time to decide what to do with her remains, my parents and I struggled with it. We were torn between the rational, less expensive choice of having her body put in the city's "pet cemetery" or paying a relatively expensive fee to have her body cremated.

Initially, my parents and I decided to have Lexi placed in the cemetery. We reasoned, after all, she was a dog. But after finding out the so-called "pet cemetery" was simply a landfill of dead animals, with no markers for the deceased pets, I decided I wanted her to be cremated instead. Was this decision rational? No, of course not. But I didn't care. Lexi wasn't just a dog, she was MY dog and a loving part of our family – too special to be thrown in a landfill.

Ironically, when I called my mom to tell her I had changed my mind, she was already at the vet's office, making arrangements to have Lexi cremated. We both had been thinking and feeling the exact same way! She later told me that on her way to the vet, Erv called her, telling her to have Lexi cremated and that he would pay for it if need be.

Although I don't think it personally mattered to Erv how Lexi's remains were handled, he knew how much Lexi meant to me. Despite me originally agreeing to have her body placed in the pet cemetery, he knew it wasn't what I ultimately wanted. And the fact that he had not only gone so far as to call Mom about it, but also offered to pay the fee, meant the world to me. *(However, I probably should've put emphasis on the word offered, because the chance of him actually paying for it was slim to none given his infamous "payment history.")*

I went to Huntsville about a week later to pick up Lexi's cremated remains from the vet's office and to finally have some sort of closure. Her ashes were placed in a small cherry wood box with an engraved plate that read, "In Loving Memory [of] Lexi."

On my way back to Atlanta the next day, I got pulled over for speeding. When the officer asked why I was in such a hurry, I responded: *"I'm sorry. I went home [to Alabama] yesterday to pick up my dog. Now, I'm just trying to get home and hopefully get some rest. Now that I have closure."*

When I mentioned *"my dog,"* I pointed to the wooden box in my front seat. Although the officer didn't verbally express his sympathy, it was written all over his face. *(He had to have been a dog owner himself, as that is the only way one could relate.)* He then responded: *"Ma'am, just slow down a little bit. Make sure you get there safely."* And even though I was well over the speed limit, no citation was given. I remember thanking my little four-legged angel for that blessing.

To this day, the box containing Lexi's remains sits on the computer desk in my den along with a couple of my favorite pictures of her; two small stuffed dog animals (a pug and a beagle); and a 20-oz Diet Coke bottle that reads: *"Share a Diet Coke with Lexi."* I am so glad my family decided to have her cremated, as I will cherish my keepsake forever. And because I feel no other dog could ever come close to filling the void of losing Lexi, I have no intentions of owning another pet dog – ever.

Lexi's passing was my first real experience with grief. I had lost both my maternal grandfather and my paternal grandmother prior to Lexi's passing, but I didn't grieve either of those losses the way I did Lexi.

Erv was my rock during that time. He helped me get through the grief and associated guilt I had been carrying about Lexi, such as not keeping her the last two years of her life; not making a better attempt to help her lose weight and get healthy; and not being at the vet's office when she had to be put down.

In the seven short years that I had Lexi, she made an impression on me and my family that will never be forgotten. Erv and I both ended up getting tattoos in her memory. He got a portrait of her face on his calf, and I got an infinity symbol containing her name with a heart and paw print on my wrist.

In hindsight, I realize that Lexi's premature passing – as devastating as it was at the time – was actually a blessing in disguise. Granted there is no comparison between the loss of a pet and the loss of a sibling, the smaller loss of Lexi in some ways prepared me for the greater loss ahead.

Secondly, losing Jason felt (and at times still feels) like too much to bear. To lose Lexi after such a tragic loss, would have certainly been unbearable. The thought alone almost is. Plus, Lexi loved Jason and would've grieved the loss as well. So, I'm glad her emotions were spared. Lastly (and probably most importantly), Lexi's untimely passing solidified one simple fact: Although we as believers of Christ may not fully understand or agree with God's timing, it is perfect, nonetheless.

THE ASPECTS OF THE PASSING

Chapter 7: The Hospital

*"The spirit of a man will sustain him in sickness,
but who can bear a broken spirit?"*
(Proverbs 18:14[*])

April 27, 2017 was a normal Thursday morning. Jason and I both had to get up early for work, so we talked and laughed as usual while preparing to leave. I remember calling him from work around 3 p.m. that afternoon, like usual. He didn't answer my call – no biggie. However, when he didn't return my call after a few hours, I decided to call him back – still no answer. At this point, I became slightly concerned, but eventually brushed it off. I assumed maybe he went to the gym straight from work.

About an hour later (around 7 p.m.), Erv called the pharmacy. When I saw his number on the caller ID, I quickly picked up the phone: *"Hey, where you been?"* He responded: *"At home,"* but his voice was so weak, I could tell something was wrong. I said: *"What's wrong with you?"* He said: *"I don't know. I'm just in so much pain."*

I responded: *"Pain!? Where!?"* He said: *"In my stomach. It's been hurting all day. I left work around 12 'cause I was hurtin' so bad."* I said: *"At 12!? Why didn't you call me?"* He said: *"It wasn't hurtin' this bad then. I thought I could just take some Pepto [Bismol] and be straight, but it didn't help. Then I tried to eat something,*

---

[*] From the New King James Version (NKJV).

thinking it might make me feel better and it didn't. I just been gettin' worse."

I said: *"You think you need to go to the hospital!? Go to the hospital!"* He responded: *"Eb, I can't drive. I'm in too much pain."* I said: *"Ok. You know I can't leave work right away. You want to me to find someone to come pick you up?"* He said: *"I don't know. I'm just in pain."* His voice was cracking.

I said: *"Ok. Let me make some phone calls. I'ma find somebody to come get you and take you to the hospital. And I'ma call my boss to get someone to cover my shift. I'll meet you there."* He agreed, and we hung up the phone. I immediately called home to tell my mom about Jason. I told her my plan. She said: *"Ok. Do that."*

The first person I called was Caleb. Although he was willing to take him, he was in the middle of a training session and couldn't leave right away. I then reached out to several other people that lived in the Stone Mountain area, but no one answered my call. I finally reached out to one of my pharmacy technicians who was fond of both myself and Jason.

My technician was willing to pick him up and take him, but it would probably be at least an hour or so before she could make it across town to Stone Mountain. Lastly, I reached out to my supervisor and district manager (DM), in an attempt to alert them of the situation at hand. I was able to reach the DM, who told me she'd try her best to find someone to relieve me.

I called home to let my mom know my technician was going to pick up Jason and take him to the hospital. She was relieved. But when I told her it might be an hour or so before she reached him, she told me to just go ahead and call an ambulance to pick him up. After I called her originally, she called Jason to check on him for herself. By the sound of his voice, she said he couldn't wait an hour.

I agreed and called Erv back. I told him I was going to call an ambulance to pick him up. I asked if he'd be able to let them in when they arrived, or would they need to force entry. He said he could let them in, but he didn't want to have to rely on them to secure the house before leaving. So instead, he was going to lock the house and wait for them in his car. I said okay and told him to call me once the ambulance arrived, so I'd know which hospital he was going to.

After hanging up with him, I called 911 for an ambulance. I then called my technician to tell her we decided to call an ambulance instead and to thank her for her effort. I also followed up with the DM, letting her know that I had called an ambulance and that I would try to stay until closing time (9 p.m.), but I couldn't promise anything. Shortly after, Erv called me, letting me know the ambulance had arrived and which hospital they were going to carry him to.

It wasn't long before another pharmacist showed up to the pharmacy to relieve me. I had already packed my things and immediately left when she arrived. While in route to the hospital, Erv called me: *"Where are you?"* I let him know I was on my way and that I'd be there soon.

I arrived at the hospital emergency room around 9 p.m. Soon after signing in, I saw a triage nurse wheeling Jason back to the waiting area. The pain in his face was heartbreaking. After being seated, I asked what all had occurred since he made it to the hospital. He said: *"Not much. They just took some blood, [checked] my blood pressure, and made me pee in a cup. Sh*t like that."* I said: *"Ok. Well, hopefully they'll call you back soon."*

Boy, was I wrong. We sat in that waiting area for hours. Erv went from being frustrated and impatient to being angry. As bad as he was hurting, he couldn't understand why it was taking so long for him to get help. I tried my best to comfort and console him. Meanwhile, I made constant trips to the front desk, asking how much longer it would be. I begged them to expedite the process, but to no avail. All their answers were vague and unpromising. We ended up waiting several hours before Erv was seen.

The Emergency Room

Erv was admitted into the emergency room (ER) early that Friday morning. It was a little after midnight. Once in the ER we subconsciously reverted to our childhood ways. Even though he was still fully capable of speaking for himself, whenever a nurse or P.A. would ask him a question, Erv just looked at me, and I answered[*] – because I was my brother's keeper.

Once in the ER, Jason was finally given medicine to help alleviate some of his pain, before initial testing and treatments were begun. The first treatment the P.A. suggested was to suction Jason's stomach, assuming this would help break up or remove any objects or food particles that may be causing the discomfort.

This procedure was a painful experience for Jason and a painful sight for me, as the tube had to be placed up his nose, down his throat, and into his stomach. In addition to the physical pain caused by the

---

[*] P.A. is the abbreviation for a Physician's Assistant.

placement of the tubing, it also triggered his gag reflex, causing him to repeatedly vomit (into a bag) as the tube was being put into position.

Unfortunately, the suction process was unsuccessful. Only gastric juices were removed, and Erv still complained about the pain he was experiencing. As a result, the P.A. ordered a CT scan, assuming the pain may be associated with his gallbladder. If that was the case, a minor surgical procedure would occur to remove it.

The CT scan revealed no problem with his gallbladder. Instead, it revealed a small bowel obstruction – a blockage in his small intestine. At this point, Erv was admitted into the hospital, as he would now have to undergo a major emergency surgery.

It was a little after 2 a.m. by the time the surgeon arrived. After reviewing the results of the scan, he came to Erv's room to speak with us and explain the procedure. Essentially, he would be opening Jason's small intestine; removing the blockage; and closing the area back up. Hopefully, without having to remove a large part of his intestine during the process.

Upon describing the surgery and answering my questions, the doctor's surgical team prepared Erv for surgery. Once he was ready to enter the operating room (OR), I was escorted to the nearest waiting area by one of the OR nurses.

After a few hours, the surgeon came to the waiting area to give me an update on how the surgery went and how Erv was doing. He informed me that although the surgery went well, the problem was worse than he had originally suspected.

Once inside, he realized that Jason's intestine was twisted, almost like a rope. Additionally, some areas were twisted so tightly, they had become necrotic. In other words, there was no blood flow to these areas, causing the cells and surrounding to tissue to die. Thus, explaining the intense pain Jason felt.

As a result, the surgeon had to perform a bowel resection, removing the necrotic parts of the intestine. In addition, Jason developed a minor infection due to the surgery. Therefore, the surgeon didn't want to completely close the incisions (his intestines) until the infection was cleared. That being the case, Jason would have to undergo a second procedure in the next three to four days.

Nonetheless, the surgeon assured me that Jason was in recovery and doing well. Once out of recovery, he would be moved to the intensive care unit (ICU) for close monitoring until the second surgery was to be completed. He then suggested that I go home and get some rest.

After speaking with the doctor, I immediately called home to update my parents. They were relieved that the surgery went well. My mom made plans to come into town later that morning. My dad decided to go on to work, with plans to come to Atlanta the next day.

I left the hospital around 5:30 a.m. At that point, not only had I been up for about 24 hours, but it also had been over 12 hours since I had eaten or drank anything. Practically starving, I stopped by the local 24-hour McDonald's. I ate my food in the car and once home, I crashed within minutes of hitting my bed.

I only managed to sleep for a few hours before waking back up. Soon after, I called my mom to see how much ground she had covered in her trip to Atlanta. She informed me that she was nearby, so I decided to wait for her before returning to the hospital.

The ICU

Upon returning to the hospital later that Friday morning, I was so glad my mom was with me. Seeing Jason in the ICU was heartbreaking, a sight that may have been unbearable on my own. He was under sedation, and his eyes were rolling around in his head. It also seemed like a million tubes and lines were coming in and out of different areas of his body, the most noticeable one being the gigantic tracheal tube going down his throat to assist with his breathing.

In addition to the tubes and lines, I noticed that restraints had been put on his wrists. I asked his nurse why the medical team felt the need to restrain him. She said he had been so agitated upon awakening in recovery that he pulled his central line out of his arm. And even with the restraints, due to his physical strength, he was still able to pull at other lines, resulting in the need to keep him under mild sedation.

After seeing Jason, Mom called Dad, suggesting he come in town once he got off work that afternoon versus waiting until Saturday. Soon after, I contacted Erv's friends, Reu and Matt via group text to let them know Erv was in the ICU, asking them to send up a prayer for his recovery. The three of them were like brothers, so I wanted them to be the first to know. I also messaged several of Jason's other friends, my friends, and our mutual friends asking everyone to keep him and our family lifted in prayer.

Soon after receiving my message, Reu called me back asking for more details and the location of the hospital, as he and Matt happened to be together at the time and were going to head directly there. Not too long afterward, they arrived at the hospital.

Upon seeing Erv, the hurt in their hearts was immediately evident. But since he was still sedated and, by that time, some of our aunts had arrived from Alabama, they decided not to stay long. Before leaving, they hugged me; thanked me for contacting them; and asked me to keep them posted on his status.

Shortly after Matt and Reu left, Erv came to. The nurse advised that we visit him one or two at a time, as not to overwhelm or agitate him. My mom and I were the first to see him. Although he couldn't talk (as he was still intubated with the tracheal tube), we could tell he was happy to see us.

I asked him to nod his head if he could hear me. When he did, I told him the doctor said the surgery went well. I also told him that Reu and Matt had come by to see him and that Dad was on his way, riding with some of our cousins. Lastly, I told him I loved him. My mom then said a few words to Jason as well, also expressing how much she loved him.

When my mom and I finished speaking to him, Jason then tried his best to tell us something. He was moving his mouth, but due to the tracheal tube, we couldn't read his lips. He was also motioning with his hand, but because he was still under restraint, we couldn't determine exactly where he was pointing.

My mom and I desperately started blurting out any- and everything we thought he could possibly be trying to tell us, all to no avail. He shook his head no to everything we said. When we realized that he was getting agitated and tired, we summoned the nurse.

When she arrived in the room, Jason mouthed his concern to her while motioning his hand. Just as he had done with us. She guessed correctly on the first try: He needed to have a bowel movement. I was relieved and upset all at the same time.

I was glad she understood his need and that it wasn't of an urgent nature or associated with him being in any additional pain. However, I was disappointed that I was unable to figure it out. All our lives I've been able to confidently speak on my brother's behalf, and it seemed like the one time in which he needed me to do so the most, I couldn't.

Nonetheless, the nurse told him to handle his business in the bed, and they would clean up everything when he was finished. Erv did not like the idea of that at all. He had always been very particular about keeping himself clean, sometimes taking multiple showers a day, so the thought of having to sit in his own feces was disturbing. It was evident on his face. My mom and I felt sorry for him, but he didn't have a choice.

Soon after that episode, Erv became agitated once again and started pulling his restraints. As a result, he had to be put back under sedation, only this time he was put into a medically induced coma. His blood pressure had dropped so low at this point, that the medical team couldn't risk him pulling out another central line, as they probably wouldn't be able to establish another one if the current one was to be removed.

Unfortunately, Jason was still in a coma by the time our dad arrived at the hospital that evening. After closing the curtain to Jason's room, I could see the pain in my dad's eyes as he sat beside my mom. It was devastating. At that point, all I could do was pray for my dad's strength and Jason's recovery. I knew, ultimately, no other consolation could be provided to my parents after seeing their son in a vegetative state. As his sister, I felt helpless. So, I couldn't begin to imagine how they felt as parents.

Everyone besides our cousins, who traveled with my dad, spent the night in the hospital with Jason. It was me, our parents, and three of our aunts. We were all crammed in the small waiting area adjacent to Jason's room in the ICU, allowing us to look behind the curtains at him or easily step into his room to be with him.

Since my parents and aunts occupied the cushioned furniture in the waiting area, I remember putting two wooden end tables together to lie on, eventually falling asleep during the wee hours of the next morning. The next thing I remember was my Aunt Brenda tapping me on my shoulders, frantically saying: *"Ebony, get up! You've gotta get up! Get up!"* I jumped up and ran to the opening connecting the two rooms. When I pushed the curtain back, I instantly started crying and saying: *"God, no! No!!!"*

Jason had coded. In other words, he had gone into cardiac arrest. The medical team had been alerted to his room and had begun resuscitative efforts, cycling through chest compressions. When a petite nurse began her cycle of compressions, I noticed Jason's chest was barely moving.

I begged one of the members of the medical team to let me do a round of compressions, saying: *"She's not pressing hard enough! I'm stronger than her. That's my brother. I can help, please! I'm a pharmacist. I'm a licensed CPR provider. Please!"* She forcefully responded: *"Ma'am, stand back!"* while gently pushing me back into the waiting area, closing the curtain.

I sat down on one of the tables in which I had been sleeping and began to pray. Everyone in the room was praying. And in what seemed like an eternity, although it was only a matter of minutes, I heard someone on the medical team say: *"We have a heartbeat!"* I, along with everyone else in the waiting area, immediately started thanking God and crying tears of joy.

Soon after, one of the doctors came to speak with us, describing what had happened and why. Jason's blood pressure had dropped very low – to an undetectable level. In addition, the infection the surgeon had originally mentioned to me, had become septic, spreading into his bloodstream. Nonetheless, with him being so young and otherwise healthy, she was still very optimistic about his recovery.

The doctor even expressed how the muscles in his chest allowed them to forcefully compress without causing any additional harm – for example, breaking a rib. My family was relieved to hear the positive prognosis. Yet and still, we continued to pray for Jason's health and recovery. In fact, I've never prayed that hard in my life. I was desperate, begging God to restore my brother's health.

Afterward, I remember sitting at Jason's bedside, tears running down my face as I looked at his comatose body. I then began speaking to him, not caring if he could hear me or not. I told him how much I loved him and how I was still praying for him. I told him what had happened to him with the code and how that big muscular chest he took so much pride in helped save his life.

I reminded him of how strong he was – mentally and physically – and that he would get through this. Lastly, I remember telling him he HAD to get through this, referring to the fact that he always joked with the three of us about how he was going to outlive us all and the different things he'd say at each of our funerals. I also reminded him that he always said he was going to grow so old that everyone would read about him in the paper: *"Mr. Jason Ervin, a native of Huntsville, AL, turned 107 years old today!"*

I don't know how much time had passed after I left Jason's bedside, but it couldn't have been more than an hour or two, before my family heard over the loudspeaker: *"Code Blue! ICU Room 4! Code Blue!"* Jason had coded once again. Our family immediately began crying and praying.

I remember my mom eventually left the waiting room and went into the hallway. Everyone else remained in the room, praying. Although it took longer than the first code, our prayers were eventually answered. A heartbeat was established.

I ran out of the waiting room to find my mom and share the good news with her. She had gone to the main waiting area down the hall. When I opened the door with tears down my face, she started saying: *"No! No! No!"* assuming the worst, not knowing my tears were tears of joy.

I grabbed my mom and responded: *"They found a heartbeat!"* *"Huh?"* she replied. Disbelief was written on her face. I repeated: *"Mom! They found a heartbeat!"* We both started shouting and praising God, both crying tears of joy that our prayers had been answered. My mom then left the waiting area to go check on my dad.

It is important to note, although all of us began intensely praying once Jason coded for the second time, my prayer had changed. I was no longer praying for Jason's recovery. I was simply praying for God's will to be done, regardless of what that was.

Being in the medical field myself, I knew his body couldn't continue to withstand the medical team's resuscitative efforts. I was also familiar with sepsis. So, I knew if the doctors didn't get the infection under control, Jason's overall health would quickly begin to decline, resulting in a diminished quality of life if he did survive.

Lastly, being a pharmacist, I knew something wasn't right in terms of Jason's comatose state. The medical team had discontinued his sedatives several hours before, yet Jason hadn't woken up. And even if the sepsis had progressed and decreased his kidney function, by that time, the drug still should have cleared his system. He should've already come to. Nonetheless, God had answered my prayer, and I was happy for that.

Soon after leaving, my mom returned to the waiting area to come get me. Since I was a medical professional, she wanted me to talk to the medical team on their behalf regarding the next steps in Jason's care. I ended up speaking with the nephrologist. As I had speculated, Jason's kidneys were failing due to the septic infection. The doctor gave me two options: They could withdraw care or attempt to do dialysis. As far as I was concerned, withdrawing care wasn't an option. So, I asked to hear more about the dialysis procedure.

Performing dialysis was a catch-22 because of Jason's blood pressure, which was still undetectable at that time. To perform dialysis, his blood pressure had to not only be detectable, but also be at a certain number. However, even if his blood pressure reached the minimum threshold, performing dialysis could still, subsequently, drop his blood pressure to a fatal level.

I explained the dilemma to my parents. My mom responded: *"My God! We need a miracle."* I agreed: *"Yes Lord, please,"* before returning to the doctor. He asked how we wanted to proceed. I asked if they could try once more to take Jason's blood pressure, as we would like to try dialysis. He agreed. And low and behold, when the nurse took Jason's pressure, not only did it show up on the machine, it was several points above the minimum threshold. God had answered our prayers yet again.

When the nephrologist went to prepare his team for dialysis, I left the personal waiting room and went to the larger one down the hall. I called my best friend Alex to update her on Jason's status; to tell her about my changed prayer; and to ask her to continue praying for us.

Soon after hanging up with her, my mom entered the room. I told her I felt like our prayer needed to change. We needed to agree and start praying for God's will to be done, instead of solely praying for Jason's recovery. She agreed, acknowledging that his body couldn't continue to endure what he had been going through. She left to go talk with my dad.

She came back to the waiting area to tell me Dad agreed. Not even five minutes later we heard: *"Code Blue! ICU Room 4! Code Blue!"* My mom and I fell to the floor in agony, crying and screaming. A few minutes later my dad came to the waiting area and said: *"He's gone."*

I remember going back to the room a few minutes later to get one more look at my baby brother. The medical team had cleaned him up well. All the tubes and lines had been removed from his body. He looked so peaceful. His body didn't look worn or battered. He didn't look like all he had been through over the last 24-36 hours. I still thank God for that.

I never imagined I'd be leaving that hospital without my brother. I'm pretty sure it never crossed Erv's mind either. In hindsight, I believe Erv struggled with God about leaving us. He recovered from that first code so quickly. It was almost as if he was saying: *"Nah God, I ain't ready, and they ain't ready. I can't go right now."* After the second one, it was like he said: *"I'm ready, but they ain't. So, I still can't go just yet."* Finally, when the three of us agreed upon our new prayer, and Erv coded that last time, it was as if he said: *"Ok God, I know they're gonna be ok now. I can go."*

God's will for Jason had been done. On Saturday, April 29, 2017, shortly after 8 a.m., He called my brother home to be with Him in Heaven. On April 29, 2017, Jason went from being my baby brother to my guardian angel. Now, he's my keeper.

After viewing Jason's body, I went to the hallway and began texting everyone Jason or I was close to, alerting them of his passing. Several people attempted to call me immediately after receiving the news. I remember answering each call, crying hysterically, trying my best to talk and answer their questions. But I was hyperventilating, often only having the strength to say: *"He's dead! My brother's dead! I can't talk. Just text me,"* in between breaths.

There were two interactions, however, that I vividly remember. The first interaction was with Caleb. He was one of the first people I recall texting. However, after messaging him, I instantly realized he was in the middle of leading a *Burn 1000* class.

Caleb called me right when class was over at 9 a.m. I remember him saying as his voice cracked: *"Hey, umm, I was just calling to check on you."* I remember hysterically responding back: *"Caleb, he's dead! Jason is dead!"* before handing my phone off to our friend Allison, who had arrived at the hospital by that time.

I was later told, that upon reading my text during class, Caleb immediately collapsed to the ground. When the class came to his side, he told them Jason had passed away. In memory of Jason, they tried to continue working out but struggled, as everyone who knew him was heartbroken.

The second interaction involved my most recent ex at the time, Ted.[*] Although he and I hadn't spoken in months at the time of Jason's passing, he was still one of the first people I notified. He and I had dated for years, so he knew, firsthand, the relationship I had with my brother. So, despite our lack of communication, he immediately came to the hospital, arriving around the same time as two of my friends from work.

Ted stayed by my side the entire time my family remained at the hospital. He was my rock. He held me as I cried on his chest. And anytime I collapsed to the floor in hysteria, he quickly picked me up. Additionally, if I needed something, like a cup of water, he rushed to go get it. Ted was nothing short of amazing that day (and in the months to come). I was so thankful to have his support.

[*] Name has been changed.

Chapter 8: The Funeral

"They all cried as they embraced and kissed him good-bye.
They were sad most of all because…
they would never see him again."
(Acts 20:37-38[*])

Upon arriving back at my house Saturday afternoon, several of mine and Jason's friends and coworkers stopped by to visit myself and my parents, expressing their condolences for our loss. My cousins who had brought my dad in town the day before also returned. Although my parents and other family members went back to Huntsville Sunday morning, I decided to stay in Atlanta an additional day.

Soon after my family left, my three best friends from Huntsville – Alex, Erica, and Katrenia – arrived at my house. I was so surprised, yet happy to see them. They spent a couple hours with me before getting back on the road. Less than an hour after they left, Allison and some of mine and Jason's other Trendsetter friends stopped by to visit. I remember feeling so thankful for the all the love shown by our friends within those first 24-36 hours of Jason's passing.

Between word of mouth and social media, the news of Jason's passing spread like wildfire. Never in my life, had I received so many phone calls, text messages, and Facebook notifications. It was almost overwhelming. Although I won't go into detail about all the things

[*] From the New Living Translation (NLT).

that were said or expressed during this time, I would like to share a few of the interactions.

The first two interactions came in the form of Facebook messages, one from someone I knew and the other from someone I didn't. The person I knew sent: *"Hey, heard about Jason. What happened?"* as if he had simply broken a limb or something, you know? As if he weren't deceased. She showed no sympathy for my loss, and therefore, received no response from me.

I tried not to let the following message bother me, because I didn't know the person personally. But in hindsight, the fact that I didn't know her only made it worse. After obviously seeing the posts and comments about Jason's passing on my page, this person (an adult) sent: *"Hey, is your brother dead?"* Your reaction upon reading that is probably similar to the one I had: *"Seriously!? What the hell???"* Needless to say, she didn't get a response either.

This last interaction was with a close friend of mine via phone and was, by far, the worst interaction yet. In fact, the worst interaction period. Upon learning the news of Jason's passing, my friend called me that Sunday afternoon. When I answered the phone, she cried: *"Ebony, no!?"* Once I confirmed that Jason had indeed passed away the previous morning, she became hysterical, crying uncontrollably. In fact, she was crying so hard that I eventually found myself trying to console her!

Once she calmed down a bit, my friend then went on to exclaim: *"Oh my God. And he was so fine! Girl, I never told you, but I wanted to have sex with him so bad! And I know it woulda been* *good! Now, I'll never know!"* She sighed before continuing: *"Now, I guess I'll just have to fantasize about it..."*[*]

Now, if you were in shock while reading that, just imagine how I felt hearing it. This was my brother she was talking about – my *deceased* brother – whom my family hadn't even buried yet. And after briefly expressing her condolences, these were her choice words.

I was in complete and utter disbelief. In fact, I still am. I mean, to be honest, her saying that to me would've been inappropriate and awkward had Jason still been alive. So in his absence, it was beyond disrespectful. I was completely speechless. Our conversation ended almost immediately after that.

I chose to share these particular interactions because, to this day, I still can't understand how or why a person would assume or think it would be okay to say such things to someone in my position. Someone who has literally JUST experienced the biggest loss or tragedy of her life.

Now, I'm sure these people didn't mean any harm. In fact, the ones who sent the Facebook messages probably meant well or were simply concerned. Yet and still, I'm reminded of the saying: *"It's not what you say. It's how you say it."* However, in terms of the phone conversation, it was what she said. There was no correct way to say that. It just shouldn't have been said – ever.

At any rate, I'd like to end this section on a high note. So, I want to mention a special Facebook post (video) that was made that weekend in honor of Jason. It was by our trainer, Caleb. The video

---

[*] FYI: This is a condensed, loose quote – the PG-13 version of what was actually said.

began with footage of Jason (and I) working out at Trendsetter, TFC, and anywhere else he may have had us.

The footage was followed by different pictures of Jason while working out and with members of the gym. It ended with a video clip of Jason dancing in the gym, which he was known for doing. Everything about the post, including the kind words in Caleb's caption and the music he selected to play in the background, was beautiful. In preparing to write this paragraph, I watched the video again and cried as if it were my first time seeing it.

Huntsville

I left for Huntsville Monday morning. Although the funeral wasn't scheduled until Thursday, I didn't have much time to spend or spare in Atlanta. My mom put me in charge of selecting the pictures for the slideshow we were planning to play before the start of the funeral as well as creating the obituary.

I began working on the verbiage for the obituary almost immediately after arriving home. My mom gave me a list of key points to include, so I had no problems getting started. Soon after I had my thoughts together, my cousin Shantel happened to stop by. So, I got her to help with the finishing touches. I knew our final draft of the obituary was perfect, because it brought tears to my mom's eyes as she read it. Once finished she said: *"Yep, that's my baby."*

Upon learning of Jason's passing, numerous people had inquired about the cause of death and funeral arrangements. So, after completing the obituary, I decided to make a post on Facebook formally announcing his passing. In addition, I provided a brief description of the events that led to his passing and thanked everyone for their love and support. I ended the post by sharing his funeral arrangements.

The feedback on the post was incredible. It received more likes, comments, and shares than anything I (or Jason) had ever posted in the past. It warmed my heart to know that my brother and I were so loved and cared about, and that so many people had my family and I in their thoughts and prayers.

In addition to writing the obituary and Facebook post, I also had to write a speech upon arriving home, as I had planned to speak at the funeral. However, everyone, including my parents, seemed surprised that I wanted to speak about Jason. Some people even questioned my ability to do so, asking if I'd have the strength to stand up and talk.

I admit this was a valid concern. Yet and still, considering Jason was my one and only sibling, not speaking at his funeral wasn't an option in my mind. Nobody knew that boy better than me. Not even my parents. So, there was no way in the world he was going to be eulogized and buried without ME saying something first. As Erv would say: *"Nah bruh, that wasn't gonna happen."*

As far as my strength or ability to do so? I wasn't worried about that at all. Now, I expected to be nervous, simply because I would be speaking before a crowd. But my ultimate ability to relay my message and express the things I wanted to say about my brother? I knew, without a shadow of a doubt, that God and my angel would have my back on that. Even if I were weak every other minute of that day, for those few minutes, I was confident I'd be strong.

The Funeral

Jason's funeral was held Thursday, May 4th, at 12 noon at Progressive Union, the church he and I had grown up in. His body had been prepared by Royal Funeral Home in Huntsville. The funeral director and staff arrived at my parent's house at 10:30 a.m. that morning to pick up my family and begin the funeral procession to the church.

My grandmother and Jason's "brothers," Reu and Matt, rode in the limousine with me and my parents. Some other members of my family traveled in a second limousine. Everyone else who had gathered at my parents' house followed the limos.

Upon arriving at the church, my family and I exited our vehicles and began lining up to enter the sanctuary. My parents led the procession. I followed behind them with a single red rose in hand, escorted by Reuben and Matthew on either arm. My grandmother was next in line, followed by the rest of my family.

As my parents approached Jason's casket, my mom began to stumble. My dad and an usher had to hold her up so she could continue. Upon arriving at the casket, my mom began screaming: *"My baby!"* then *"Jason!"* The agony in her voice was gut-wrenching. She placed her hand on his chest and spoke her last words to the body of her baby boy, while my dad stood behind her crying. Once finished, she kissed him. Then the two of them took their seat on the first pew.

I was next. I left my escorts and approached the casket alone. This would be my first time seeing Jason's prepared body, as I chose not to view him during visiting hours at the funeral home. He looked so handsome, so peaceful. His head was freshly shaven, and his beard was perfectly lined – just the way he would've wanted it. Diamond studs were in each of his ears.

My mom had put me in charge of his clothing. Knowing Erv had never been one to dress up, I decided to dress him in chef attire. I selected a charcoal grey chef coat, in which he had had his name – *"Chef Jason Ervin"* – embroidered in red lettering. The outfit went perfectly with the beautiful ebony and charcoal casket my mom had selected and the large bouquet of red roses I had chosen as the casket flower.

Upon arriving at the casket, I placed the rose I had been carrying across his chest, resting my hand there as I cried and spoke my final words to the flesh of my baby brother. I can't recall all the words that were said, but I know I ended by expressing how much I was going to miss him and how much I loved him. I then kissed his forehead and took my seat next to my parents.

When my grandmother reached the casket, she too screamed in agony for her grandson. Her sister, my great aunt Pearl, held her for support. Once she left to take her seat, the remainder of the processional viewed the body, many of them stopping to hug my parents and I on the way to their seats.

A couple minutes later, I realized the funeral staff had begun to lower Jason's body into the casket, preparing to close it. I quickly ran back up to the casket, hovering and crying over my brother's body. Almost immediately after, my parents joined me. All three of us were hovering over Jason's body and crying. While at the casket, I almost fell to my knees several times, weak at the thought of never seeing my brother again.

My parents went back to their seat shortly after joining me. However, I remained at the casket for a few more moments, before finally being helped to my seat by my one of my cousins. The funeral staff then proceeded to close the casket, as the choir began singing their first selection. By the time the choir's song ended, Jason's casket was closed with the beautiful arrangement of roses sitting on top of it.

The choir selection was proceeded by the opening prayer and scripture readings from both the old and new testaments of the bible. After the final scripture reading, the choir sang a second song before the reflections portion of the ceremony began.

There were three reflections planned on the program: one from Reuben, one from Jason's other friend, A.J., and mine. Reuben's speech was very emotional and from the heart. He shared some of the fond memories and experiences he (and Matt) had with Erv over the years, his voice often cracking as he fought back tears. The love he had for my brother, *his* brother, was evident. Unfortunately, A.J. did not arrive from Atlanta in time to give his speech. So, I followed Reuben.

My reflection lasted roughly ten minutes. Although not an original part of my speech, I began by sharing a funny experience that occurred prior to me taking the podium to speak: As I was making my way across the aisle and up the stairs to the podium, I could hear Erv saying: *"Eb, man. Cut all that cryin' out! Pull yourself together now. So, you can put some respec' on my name!"* After the crowd and I shared a brief laugh, I asked them to give me a minute to *"pull myself together, so I could put some respec' on my brother's name."*

I began my speech by detailing a few humorous events from our childhood and how they coincided with some of the events at the hospital the previous week. I then went on to make it clear that I didn't choose to speak about Jason to mourn my loss. I stated, *"I have the rest of my life to do that."* Instead, I wanted to do the exact opposite. I wanted to celebrate his life, saying: *"because if Jason didn't do anything else, he lived!"*

I then went on to detail some of the events and interactions – both humorous and sincere – from our adulthood in Atlanta, sharing the ways he and I differed in terms of how we lived our lives. I then went on to express my desire and plan to live a happier and more fulfilled life, like Jason. I concluded by encouraging the audience to not only do the same, but more importantly, to *"be like my angel. Be like Jason. While you're alive, just live."*

Although I didn't notice it during the funeral, upon watching the DVD of the ceremony (in preparation for this part of the book), I noticed that during my speech, not only did my parents smile, but at times they laughed, which warmed my heart to see. In hindsight, I'm glad to know that I was able to temporarily lift their spirits on one of the worst days of their lives, second only to April 29th, the day of Jason's passing.

After I finished speaking, surprisingly, one of Jason's former Sodexo supervisors (from one of his earlier corporate positions) came to the podium to speak. She expressed how well-loved Jason was in Atlanta by her and others he had worked with. She followed with a fond and funny memory she had of working with him.

Although I didn't know it at the time, she had also attended the event Jason catered just before passing. She remembered telling him how happy she was to see he had *"come into his own as a chef."* She shared with us how great the food was and how proud she was of him. She ended by expressing her grief and sympathy for our family.

The reflections were followed by the reading of two resolutions. The first resolution was sent from my grandmother's church, The First Community Missionary Baptist Church in Cleveland, Ohio. The second resolution was sent from Pastor Curney and New Mercies Christian Church in Atlanta (Lilburn, GA). The resolutions were proceeded by *"Words of Comfort"* by our pastor at Progressive Union, Wayne P. Snodgrass.

Pastor Snodgrass' message was entitled, *"There Is Life in The Valley."* His message was derived from Psalms 23:4 which reads: *"Yea, though I walk through the valley of the shadow of death, I will fear no evil; For You are with me; Your rod and Your staff, they comfort me."**

He started the message by saying that *"death never offers a perfect time"* to occur in our lives. But in addition to God, time itself, will be the best remedy for our current pain and suffering. Using himself as an example, he assured us that with time, our discomfort will lessen. He also suggested that we rely on our memories, family and friends, and fellow saints to help us during the grieving process.

He concluded his message by encouraging us to find comfort in knowing that even though we are experiencing darkness – or, the shadow of [Jason's] death – that God is with us and will not leave our side. Also, while in this "valley" of darkness, with God's help, there can and will be continued life. He closed by reminding us that Jason

---

* From the New King James Version (NKJV).

had been saved and was now with God. Thus, free from any pain, suffering, harm, or evil.

Pastor Snodgrass' message was followed by a solo selection. I had reached out to a childhood friend whom Jason and I had grown up with at Progressive Union. I had always loved to hear him sing. So, he was the first person that came to mind when planning the funeral. He chose to sing *"His Eye Is on The Sparrow,"* and he sung it beautifully. I probably had just as many tears in my eyes watching and listening to him on the DVD as I did the day of the funeral.

The ceremony ended with a closing prayer by one of my mom's dear friends, Beverly. After the prayer, the funeral home staff prepared for the recessional. Our family had been given *so* many flowers. In addition to the flower bearers listed on the program, several of my other cousins and aunts had to help carry flowers out of the sanctuary.

The flower bearers were proceeded by the pallbearers. However, the funeral home staff were responsible for carrying (wheeling) the casket out of the sanctuary. My parents were directly behind the casket, followed by myself (escorted by Reuben and Matthew), my grandmother, and the rest of my family.

The music I selected for the recessional was a continuous loop of the chorus and bridge from Wiz Khalifa's song, *"See You Again,"* featuring Charlie Puth:

> *It's been a long day…without you, my friend.*
> *And I'll tell you all about it, when I see you again.*
> *We've come a long way…from where we began.*
> *Oh, I'll tell you all about it, when I see you again.*
> *When I see you again…*

How can we not talk about family...when family's all that we got?
Everything I went through, you were standing there by my side.
*And now you gon' be with me for the last ride.**

After the funeral, my parents and I stood outside the church for a few minutes greeting and hugging everyone that approached us. I was happy to see so many of our childhood friends as well as so many people from Atlanta. With the funeral being on a Thursday, I expected most people to be unavailable. I was surprised (and thankful) to see so many familiar faces.

The Burial

Jason was buried at Valhalla Memory Gardens in Huntsville, a private cemetery located less than 15 minutes from my parents' home. Upon arriving at the cemetery after the funeral, my family was escorted to the tent and chairs stationed at Jason's plot. My parents and I were seated directly in front of his casket.

In addition to the beautiful casket my mom selected, my parents also purchased a vault for Jason's casket to be placed in at the cemetery. Placing the casket inside the vault would protect it from any potential water damage caused by rain or snow.

Many people would deem a vault unnecessary. However, to my parents and myself, it was very necessary. The three of us always spoiled Jason and wanted him to have nothing but the best while he was living. In his absence, we felt the same way. We wanted him to have nothing but the best.

* Music from the *Furious 7* movie soundtrack.

The burial service was very brief. The funeral director began with a few kind and encouraging words and concluded with a prayer. After the prayer, the cemetery workers got in position to lower Jason's casket into the ground. At the first sound of the casket being released from its pedestal, I exited the tent and returned to the limousine. I couldn't watch them lower my brother's body into the ground. My parents arrived at the limousine shortly after I did, obviously feeling the same way about their son.

The Repass

Jason's current supervisor at Sodexo came to Huntsville to attend his funeral. He arrived in town the day before and stopped by my parents' house to meet the three of us. He spoke highly of Jason, describing the initial impression Jason made on him during his interview for the management position. He also expressed the positive impression and impact Jason left with not only his colleagues at Sodexo, but also members of the Atlanta Public Schools Systems' culinary program with whom he had been in contact or associated with.

Also, because of all the feedback received by Sodexo upon Jason's passing, his supervisor informed us that the company wanted to do something special for our family. Therefore, Sodexo covered the entire cost of the food for the repass, which wasn't a small expense.

My parents and I were shocked that despite Jason being there for only a few short months, such a grand gesture had been made on his behalf. We felt even more thankful and blessed knowing that God had placed Jason in the company of such good people during his last few months.

The repass was held at Progressive Union in the church's Family Christian Life Center. It was catered by Popeye's Louisiana Kitchen. The amount of food at the repass was unbelievable. Never in my life had I seen so much chicken in one place! In addition to the chicken, several side items were available. I remember the serving staff replenishing them from tub-sized containers. There was also a ridiculous number of cinnamon apple pies and mardis gras cheesecakes for dessert.

I ate *so* much food during and after the repass. I imagine I consumed almost as much food (if not more) in that one day, as I had in the last five days combined, considering my appetite was virtually non-existent after leaving the hospital Saturday morning. In fact, I ate so much chicken and so many biscuits and pies during that time, that it was several months before I even *thought* about eating at Popeye's. And even more time after that before I actually did.

My family ended up taking almost half of the food from the repass home with us. I remember my mom giving away 10-piece Ziploc bags of chicken and biscuits to almost anyone who stopped by to visit after the funeral. It reminded me of that famous Oprah Winfrey meme, mimicking the time she gave away all those cars on her television talk show: *"You get a bag of chicken! You get a back of chicken! Everybody gets a bag of chicken!!!"* – lol.

The Month of May

I remember feeling a sense of relief the morning after the funeral. Not because we had finally laid Jason's body to rest (because that still felt surreal), but more so because everything immediately calmed down after the funeral.

All my parents' house guests had come and gone, and we weren't expecting any additional visitors later that day. Also, my phone activity and social media notifications had finally resumed to a somewhat normal level. Plus, I had taken a six-week leave of absence from work. So, I didn't have to worry about rushing back to Atlanta.

I stayed in Huntsville for a few days before making a quick trip back to Atlanta. I had set up a meeting with my immediate supervisor and his direct report, the district manager, to address my concerns about returning to work the following month. During the meeting, I discussed the need to reduce my base weekly hours upon my return.

Given the circumstances, I knew I wouldn't be able to return to work in the capacity in which I left (as it related to time spent at the pharmacy). However, I asked to remain in my pharmacy manager position, as I felt I was still capable of performing the job.

The two of them were very sympathetic toward my situation and understood my need to spend less time at the pharmacy. They immediately approved my request. Essentially, I was no longer scheduled to work on Fridays.

This meant, on my weekends off (which occurred every other weekend), I would be away from work upon closing Thursday night at 9 p.m. until the following Monday afternoon at 2:30, which made traveling home to see my parents much more convenient. On the flip side, prior to working on the weekends, I'd have more time off throughout the week. My new schedule seemed perfect, and I was beyond grateful.

I returned to Huntsville soon after the date of my meeting. Earlier in the year, my parents had planned a trip to Cleveland, Ohio to spend Mother's Day weekend with my grandmother. Since I was off from work and could now join them, they bought an additional plane ticket, so I could tag along.

After the funeral, my cousin Kris and his wife, Whitney, had given the three of us beautiful t-shirts with Jason's obituary picture printed on the front. My parents and I decided to wear these shirts to the airport the day of our flight. When we boarded the plane, one of the flight attendants asked my mom who the young guy was in the picture. My mom told her it was her son who had recently passed away, and this was our first family trip without him. She hugged my mom and expressed her condolences.

A little while later, just before takeoff, the flight attendant located the three of us (as we were scattered on the plane) and upgraded us from coach to business class, sitting together and way more comfortably. I remember thinking: *"Wow, Erv just made it to Heaven, and he's already showing out for us!"*

Even though my mom would be spending Mother's Day with her mom, I knew she would ultimately have a hard time enjoying the day given Jason's passing. In an attempt to make her smile, even if only for a moment, I made a special post for her on Facebook. I preceded the post, with the following caption:

Mom, with our recent loss of Jason, I know this is the first of several hard Mother's Day holidays for you. So, I just want to take a moment to temporarily lift your spirits with these memories and this message: I'm so thankful for the life that you and Dad provided for me and Jason. Not only did we have everything we needed growing up, but also most of our wants and desires…especially your baby Jason.

Do you remember how I used to always say, you 'raised' me but 'loved' him? Lol, well…when I was younger, there was a hint of jealousy behind that. But now I understand. It was all a part of God's plan. Jason passed knowing how much you (and Dad) loved him. And for 30 years you got to spoil him, so find comfort in that. And know that one day, you'll get to love on your baby boy again and celebrate this and all holidays with him. We all will. In the meantime, you're stuck with me, lol.

Nonetheless, Happy Mother's Day Mom! WE love you.

Below the caption was a slideshow of pictures, beginning with moments from her youth followed by pictures of her with different combinations of the three of us (myself, my dad, and Jason). I also included pictures of her with other members of our family. The final picture was a post that Jason had made the previous year (2016). It was a cute picture of him from grade school, on which he had added: *"Happy Mother's Day Mom!!! From your Baby Boy! I Love You!!"*

My mom started out smiling and laughing as she watched the slideshow. However, she was crying by the end. Seeing the pictures was bitter-sweet, as she was reminded of all the precious memories the four of us made together and how we would no longer be able to create such memories. Nonetheless, she was thankful I had taken the time to create the slideshow. She watched it several more times that day.

Upon returning to Huntsville from Cleveland, I made another trip to Atlanta for a few days before returning to Huntsville once more for my cousin Mackenzie's high school graduation. Going back home this time was somewhat emotional for me, however, as Jason and I both had plans to attend her graduation. When I arrived at my parents' house, I realized my mom felt the same way. My coming home alone this time was difficult for her as well.

I ended up spending most of the month of May in Huntsville. During that time, the number of sympathy cards, messages, and gifts my family received was unbelievable. Not only did we receive cards and gifts from people we knew personally, but to our surprise, we received several (almost just as many) from people that we didn't know directly, or even at all. The most memorable ones came from people Jason met throughout his career path:

The first example is associated with the students and staff at the private school (Wesleyan) in which Jason had worked. We received a card from almost every class. Some of the students even took it a step further and sent their own personal cards and gifts from their home addresses.

The biggest surprise, however, was that we received a card from the dean of the school, describing the positive impression Jason made on not only the students, but also the faculty and staff. In addition, he discussed how Jason knew the majority of the students by name and how fond the students had become of him and his personality. After reading the dean's card, it was evident that Jason made a bigger impact at Wesleyan than we (or even he) realized.

Another group of cards came from the people Jason had temporarily worked and lived with in Roanoke, Virginia while training for his Chop House position. These cards came as a surprise because Jason had only known these people for a short period of time, not even a month. Yet, they had so many kind words and good things to say about him, his etiquette, and his personality.

Honestly, I probably could've written an entire chapter describing the different types of feedback we received. So many of Jason's friends, coworkers, and colleagues had stories to share about the positive impact Jason made on their lives. In short, it appeared he made or left an impression literally everywhere he went. Being his sister, I always knew Jason's personality was special. I just had no idea whatsoever that so many people would have agreed.

June and July

I returned to Atlanta around the 1st of June to begin preparing for my return to work the following week. Although I was somewhat ready to return to the pharmacy, I was also anxious about it. I knew going back to work could potentially be a positive distraction from my grief. But being in the pharmacy was also associated with fond memories of Jason, and therefore, could potentially have the opposite effect at times. Thus, exacerbating my grief.

Returning to the pharmacy ended up having its pros and cons, just as I had anticipated. During our busier times, it was a great distraction from what I was going through. However, during our slower times or in the afternoons, it wasn't. Out of habit, I picked up the phone to call Jason so many times, only to have to hang up and subsequently fight back tears.

Also, almost every time the phone read "WIRELESS CALLER" (which was often), I'd think about Jason, constantly being reminded that his number would never appear under those words again. All these things, combined with the additional stress and responsibilities associated with being pharmacy manager, eventually resulted in work solely being a hindrance to my healing process versus a help.

After being in Atlanta for about a month, I had to return to Huntsville to help my mom design Jason's grave marker. Obviously, this was an emotional experience as well. But the finalized proof was perfect.

We selected a black-cherry colored plate with gold writing. It was rectangular shaped and would lay flat in the ground. Across the top of the plate were four gold icons: a cross, a pair of overlapping hearts, a chef hat, and a microphone. In the middle of the icons (between the hearts and the hat) was a base for the flower vase, which would always contain roses. The inscription read as follows:

JASON TREMAINE ERVIN
SON. BROTHER. FRIEND. CHEF. MUSICIAN.
SEPTEMBER 10, 1986 – APRIL 29, 2017
"LONG LIVE KING ERV"

June and July of 2017 proved to be exceptionally difficult months for my parents and myself. My mom's birthday as well as Father's Day were in June. And my dad's birthday was in July. On all three of these occasions, however, I made sure my parents received two cards: one from me and one (seemingly) from or about Jason.

In addition to my dad's birthday, our annual family cruise was scheduled for July. However, given the circumstances, my mom cancelled the trip, as we no longer had plans (or desired) to go. Nonetheless, I kept my scheduled vacation days and spent this time in Alabama with them.

In addition to the adjustment I had to make at work during this time, I had to make another adjustment – involving Jason's Camaro. Upon his passing, I asked my parents to leave his car with me in Atlanta for a while. Even though I knew Jason wasn't in the house, coming home every day and seeing the Camaro in the driveway gave me a slight sense of normalcy. And normalcy was something I desperately longed for in his absence.

Although I moved Jason's car soon after he passed (to photograph it for the funeral slideshow), upon returning to Atlanta after the funeral, I couldn't even bring myself to sit in it and start the engine – let alone drive it. As a result, the battery eventually died.

And even though I knew how particular Jason was about keeping his car clean, I couldn't bring myself to wash it either, so it had no protection from the elements. My parents eventually decided to have it towed to Huntsville, so my dad could drive and maintain it.

My mom came to visit me around the end of July. Before leaving for Huntsville, she called AAA to have the Camaro towed as well. I had gone to work by the time the wrecker arrived at my house. Once the Camaro was loaded on the tow truck, my mom took a picture of it and sent it to me. Seeing it brought tears to my eyes.

I was anxious the entire ride home from work, knowing the Camaro was gone. I remember crying as I pulled into my empty driveway. Not seeing the Camaro further solidified the fact that Erv was gone. In fact, it made it seem more real than the funeral itself. And therefore, once the Camaro left – my grief settled in.

Chapter 9: The Grief

"Though I speak, my grief is not relieved;
and if I remain silent, how am I eased?"
(Job 16:6[*])

After reading various definitions of the term "grief" online, I concluded that grief can be described, or summarized, as the conflicting feelings or emotional reaction caused by the end of or change in a familiar pattern or behavior. It is a multi-faceted process that each person will handle and express differently. The severity and length of the grieving process will also vary from person to person.

Before describing the different facets and expressions of my personal grief, I'd like to share a message that was sent to me via a Facebook friend shortly after Jason's passing. Hopefully, you'll find this message as helpful as I did. As I found it to be a general, yet very accurate, description of the grieving process:

I wish I could say you get used to people dying. But I never did. I don't want to. It tears a hole through me whenever somebody I love dies, no matter the circumstances. But I don't want it to 'not matter.' I don't want it to be something that just passes. My scars are a testament to the love and the relationship that I had for and with that person. And if the scar is deep, so was the love. So be it.

---

[*] From the New King James Version (NKJV).

Scars are a testament to life. Scars are a testament that I can love deeply and live deeply…and be cut, or even gouged…and that I can heal, and continue to live, and continue to love. And the scar tissue is stronger than the original flesh ever was. Scars are only ugly to people who can't see [the bigger picture].

As for grief, you'll find it comes in waves. When the ship is first wrecked, you're drowning, with wreckage all around you. Everything floating around you reminds you of the beauty and the magnificence of the ship that was and is no more. And all you can do is float. You find some piece of the wreckage, and you hang on for a while. Maybe it's some physical thing. Maybe it's a happy memory or a photograph. Maybe it's a person who is also floating. For a while, all you can do is float. Stay alive.

In the beginning, the waves are 100 feet tall and crash over you without mercy. They come 10 seconds apart and don't even give you time to catch your breath. All you can do is hang on and float. After a while, maybe weeks, maybe months, you'll find the waves are still 100 feet tall, but they come further apart. When they come, they still crash all over you and wipe you out. But in between, you can breathe. You can function.

You never know what's going to trigger the grief. It might be a song, a picture, a street intersection, the smell of a cup of coffee. It can be just about anything, and the wave comes crashing. But in between waves, there is life.

Somewhere down the line, and it's different for everybody, you'll find that the waves are only 80 feet tall. Or 50 feet tall. And while they still come, they come further apart. You can see them coming – an anniversary, a birthday, or Christmas… You can see it coming, for the most part, and prepare yourself. And when it washes over you, you know that somehow you will, again, come out the other side. Soaking wet, sputtering, still hanging on to some tiny piece of wreckage, but you'll come out.

...The waves never stop coming, and somehow you don't really want them to. But you learn that you'll survive them. And other waves will come. And you'll survive them too. If you're lucky, you'll have lots of scars from lots of love. And lots of shipwrecks. [*]

Faith *Under* Fear

There have been several situations or circumstances in my life that have briefly shook my faith in God – for example, not originally being accepted into pharmacy school (wait-listed) and my relationship with Rob ending, resulting in my first major depressive episode. However, no other event had shaken my faith as hard as losing my brother. In fact, those other events were trivial in comparison.

Although I know God answered my family's final prayer in the hospital – to let His will be done – I later became upset, disappointed, and angry with God. After the funeral, I had no desire whatsoever to step back into a church, and my prayers became fewer and farther in between. I eventually got to the point where I pretty much stopped praying all together. In essence, I gave God the silent treatment.

My disappointment and anger weren't necessarily because God called Jason home. I understand that we all must die one day. And ultimately, I knew and believed that Jason was in a better place, Heaven. I was upset because I didn't understand why he had to be called home so early, at the tender age of 30.

It seemed like Jason was just beginning to truly live. He had just obtained his dream job and had recently solidified his ability to

[*] Author unknown.

97

complete a large-scale catering job alone, another goal and future business endeavor realized. So for the life of me, I couldn't understand why God wouldn't spare his life.

Secondly, no one on this Earth knew or understood my and Jason's relationship better than God. He's ultimately the reason our bond was so close. Therefore, I couldn't understand how or why He would allow this to happen. Why He would take my brother and best friend away from me. I felt abandoned and alone, and I blamed God.

Lastly, I was angry with God because I felt as though He had taken away so many of my sibling and family hopes and dreams. My dreams for Jason, seeing him reach his full potential as a culinarian and musician – gone. My dreams of the two of us being in each other's weddings – gone. My dreams of being an aunt to Jason's children, and him being an uncle to mine – gone. My hopes of continuing our family traditions (such as our annual cruise) for years to come – gone. My hopes of creating new family traditions that included our parents plus mine and Jason's families – gone. And the hope or dream of simply growing old with my brother – now gone.

Do I feel as though I was wrong for my feelings toward God? No, absolutely not. As children (and adults) you often get upset or angry with your parents. So, as a child of God, I felt as though I could (and had a right to be) upset with my Heavenly Father.

Similar to your relationship with your earthly parents, just because you're upset, doesn't mean you love (or believe in) them any less. You're just hurt or upset by the situation or circumstances at hand. And that hurt manifests itself as anger. But just like with your parents, your anger with God will eventually (or shall I say, hopefully) subside.

Medical Attention

Despite my history of anxiety and depression, I didn't seek much medical attention to help cope with my loss. In fact, I only visited my primary care physician once during my six weeks off from work. I was having a hard time falling asleep and staying asleep throughout the night. So, I needed a sleep aid. However, I was very particular about the kind of medicine I wanted.

Being a pharmacist, I knew the addictive potential associated with most of the popular prescription sleep aids. So, I wanted to steer clear of those. I was too afraid of becoming dependent. Being as such, I asked my doctor to prescribe generic Vistaril (hydroxyzine) – a prescription antihistamine used to treat insomnia and anxiety.

The Vistaril worked well for a while, but over time it became less and less effective. Nonetheless, I failed to revisit my doctor for any additional help with my insomnia. I ultimately decided I'd have to deal with it on my own.

I also chose not to see a psychiatrist or be restarted on antidepressant therapy. Given my experience with antidepressants in the past, I wasn't very optimistic about their ability to help with my grief. Plus, given the fact I had reached an all-time low, I was even more concerned about the potential side effects, in particular – suicidality. With Erv being deceased, I was no longer afraid to die. I didn't want to take a drug that could potentially put me over the edge.

Additionally, I preferred not to see a psychiatrist simply because I didn't care to discuss what I was going through with a stranger. Someone who didn't know anything about me, Jason, or the relationship we had. Plus, since Jason and I didn't have a normal sibling relationship, the last thing I wanted to hear were the normal, or "textbook," ways of coping with my loss.

I understand these were very close-minded opinions – as psychiatrists are medical professionals who have helped millions of people cope with their losses – but they were my opinions, nonetheless. This is also not an attempt to discourage anyone else from seeking therapy. It may be of great benefit to you. Therapy may have even been of benefit to me, had I been open to it – but I wasn't.

Lifestyle Changes

Soon after Jason passed away, I noticed certain adjustments I had to make. There were also things I could no longer seem to do or desired to do in his absence. One of the first things I can remember was the fragrance of my *Glade plug-ins* scented oil air freshener. Prior to Jason's passing, *fresh linen* was the only scent I purchased. And not just plug-ins. I also bought *fresh linen* scented candles and air and carpet fresheners.

When I returned to Atlanta after the funeral, however, I couldn't tolerate the *fresh linen* smell. It reminded me too much of Erv's presence and made my heart heavy. I immediately unplugged every plug-in in the house and later replaced them with a new scent. To this day, I have not purchased any *fresh linen* scented products.

I also stopped sleeping in my bed when I returned to Atlanta. Sleeping in my bedroom seemed too "normal" at the time. And since nothing about my life seemed normal upon losing Jason, I had no desire to sleep upstairs. I'd either sleep on the den sofa or in the guest bedroom on the main level.

I had to redecorate the guest bathroom on the main level of my home as well. Jason often used it to take showers and to get dressed, so everything about it reminded me of him. So much so, that I couldn't use it until I changed the décor.

Lastly, I no longer had the desire to do things as a family. For as long as I could remember, it had always been the four of us, so going places and doing things without Jason, just didn't feel or seem right. My parents felt the same way. So, in addition to my mom cancelling the cruise we had scheduled for that year (as that and other traditions had come to an end upon Jason's passing), we also decided not to attend the Dallas versus Atlanta football game that November.

Oddly enough, I also had a taste aversion. Besides pizza, Jason and I loved to eat chicken wings. Publix wings to be exact.[*] He introduced me to them, and I became hooked. It didn't matter if they were baked, fried, or battered – we ate them.

However, in his absence, I could no longer bring myself to purchase them. In fact, the thought of eating them would sometimes make me nauseous. Ironically, no other food – including wings from other places – had that effect on me. It was only Publix wings. And just like the *fresh linen* products, I have not purchased or eaten any wings from Publix to this day.

Going into the basement (Jason's space), however, didn't bother me at all upon returning from the funeral. I was hesitant about it immediately after he passed away. But once I arrived back in

[*] Publix is a popular local (southern) grocery store chain.

Atlanta, I had no problems going down there. Interestingly enough, going to the basement often gave me a sense of peace, so much so, that I have yet to change much about it. Everything is decorated and placed the exact same way Erv left it.

"Look for Me in Rainbows"

In preparation for the slideshow we were planning for the funeral, my mom asked me to take a picture of Jason's Camaro before leaving Atlanta to come home. I took several pictures that morning, but there was one particular picture that my mom really liked. It was something about how the sunlight was hitting his car that caught her attention. So, that was the picture I decided to use for the funeral.

As aforementioned, my cousin Shantel and I were responsible for making the obituary. When we got the proof back from the funeral home, we noticed a poem had been added on one of the pages in an effort to fill up the additional space. The poem was entitled, *Look for Me in Rainbows* and read:

> *Time for me to go now, I won't say goodbye;*
> *Look for me in rainbows, way up in the sky.*
> *In the morning sunrise, when all the world is new;*
> *Just look for me and love me, as you know I loved you.*
>
> *Time for me to leave you, I won't say goodbye;*
> *Look for me in rainbows, high up in the sky.*
> *In the evening sunset, when all the world is through;*
> *Just look for me and love me, and I'll be close to you.*

It won't be forever; the day will come and then,
My loving arms will hold you, when we meet again.

Time for us to part now, we won't say goodbye;
Look for me in rainbows, shining in the sky.
Every waking moment, and all your whole life through,
Just look for me and love me, as you know I loved you.

Just wish me to be near you,
And I'll be there with you.

After reading the poem, I took a second look at the Camaro picture I had decided to use, and low and behold, there was a rainbow in the sky! In fact, out of all the pictures I had taken, it was the only one with a rainbow in the background. I was convinced the rainbow poem being added to the obituary without our prior knowledge was an act of God, so I would be aware of Jason's presence via His acts of nature.

In the months to come, I saw several rainbows. And I believe there is no coincidence in the fact that, whenever I saw a one, it happened to be on one of my hardest days – when I needed my brother (and his presence) the most. Just like at the pharmacy, when he'd stop by the consultation window. Seeing rainbows and subsequently feeling Erv's presence, instantly gave me a sense of peace. And peace was something I desperately longed for in his absence, especially on my bad days.

The Supernatural

I had always heard that people's deceased loved ones often spoke to them. But to be honest, I never really believed it. That's why the first time Erv's spirit spoke to me, it…freaked…me…out! I literally jumped because it was crystal clear and sounded as if he was right there. I'll never forget it:

I was cleaning my bedroom prior to going home for the funeral and briefly thought to myself: *"Maybe I should move back home. I don't necessarily have anything keeping me here."* Erv instantly replied: *"Really bruh!? You really gonna move back home? To boring a** Huntsville? That's what you gone do right now!?"* – lol. With Erv practically making the decision for me, I decided to continue residing in Atlanta.

After the funeral, Erv's spirit became more and more vocal. And just like the first time, his voice would always be crystal clear. His spirit would console me, make me laugh, and give advice (both solicited and unsolicited). Just like he would if he were here. And although it seemed creepy at first, eventually, I not only got used to hearing his spirit, but welcomed it.

In addition to the rainbows and his voice, Erv would also make his presence known in other ways. The examples that I can most vividly remember were associated with my bad driving habits. When Erv was alive he'd always fuss about two things when he rode in the car with me: me not always wearing my seatbelt and texting while driving. (Please don't judge me.)

However, the very first time I attempted to drive without my seatbelt upon his passing, I couldn't. Albeit hard to describe, I remember feeling this heaviness around me. It was almost as if I was stuck in place or somewhat paralyzed until I buckled my seatbelt. I experienced that feeling every time I got in my car, until I made it a habit to put my seatbelt on at the beginning of every ride – no exceptions.

I had a similar supernatural experience whenever I'd pick up my phone to text while driving. I'd immediately drop it back in its place. I could only seem to hold it in my hand when parked or stopped at a red light. The minute my car was back in motion after being stopped, my phone would instantly fall from my hand. And like the seatbelt scenario, this occurred every time I picked up my phone to text or had it in hand while my car was in motion. It wasn't long before I broke that bad habit as well.

There were several other instances in which I could feel Erv's presence or protection, implying he truly was (and still is) my guardian angel. No one had my back like he did when he was here. And knowing that he still has my back in his absence, gives me an additional sense of comfort and security.

Everyone Is Dispensable

Immediately after Jason passed away, I developed an *"everyone is dispensable"* mentality. Besides my parents, there were NO exceptions. I felt as though, if I could manage to somehow get out of bed every morning; muster the strength to function during the day; and eventually go to bed every night, without Jason being here on Earth, then essentially, I could live without anyone. And I mean, ANYONE.

When I lost Jason, I not only lost my brother, but also my best friend. He was the one person in this world I could *always* count on, no matter what. So, the loss of any other friendship or relationship – whether it be a friend, a lover, a family member, whomever – would seem minor or trivial. I felt no other loss would compare to the loss of my brother, so no other loss was worth my energy.

I didn't have the mental or emotional vigor to reach out to people to rebuild or sustain our friendship or relationship. I simply went with the flow: If you wanted to remain or increase your presence in my life – cool. If for some reason you distanced yourself or no longer wanted to be in my life – fine. My only concern was positive energy conservation.

This is not to say that I no longer cared about the friendships or relationships I had with the people in my life, because I did. I thank God for my friends, family, and loved ones – especially those who were there to support me surrounding Jason's passing and the funeral.

However, given my fragile emotional state, if sustaining a friendship or relationship with someone in any way negatively impacted my energy or hindered my ability to find some sort of peace or happiness, then I wasn't afraid to let it (or them) go. I ultimately had to do what was best for me.

Social Media

Prior to Jason's passing, it had been several months, maybe even years, since I posted on my Instagram (IG) and Facebook accounts in any sort of regular fashion. However, in Jason's absence I decided to become more active on both accounts.

My posts were not only another outlet to express my grief, but also provided another way for me to honor Jason and his memory. Since Jason's IG handle was @KingErv, anytime I made a post related to him, I'd be sure to add #LongLiveKingErv in the caption.

My posts (particularly on IG) were also a means for my friends and loved ones to check on me without having to call or text. I assured them if I was actively posting, more than likely, I was doing okay. However, if I went more than three consecutive days without making a post, it was safe to assume I was probably going through a "rough patch" and could use the additional support.

I must say, certain friends caught on to that trend *quickly*. If I went three days without posting, I could expect to hear from them on day number four. So much so, that if I received a text from one of them, I instantly would check my page to see when I last made a post. And nine times out of ten, my last post would say *"3 days ago."*

Lastly, increasing my social media presence simply gave me something to do. It was a positive distraction from my grief. In fact, I was so particular about the things I decided to share (especially if it pertained to Erv) that I spent more time than I probably should've preparing my posts. In hindsight, it's safe to say I had become somewhat obsessed with posting.

Tattoos and Paraphernalia

Two to three weeks prior to Jason's passing, I was having a conversation with one of my pharmacy technicians about tattoos. She was thinking about getting her first tattoo and decided to ask my opinion about them. In particular, she asked if I thought they were painful. My response: *"Yes! And anyone who tells you anything different is either lying or has a high threshold for pain."*

She then asked if I was done getting tattoos. I responded: *"Yes!"* But after a moment, I said: *"Well, wait. I take that back. There is one exception. Heaven forbid, but if something were to happen to Jason while we were still young, I'd get a portrait of his face tattooed on [the inside of] my forearm."* After reading that, I already know what you're thinking. The irony is absolutely crazy, right!? I mean, seriously. What…were…the…*odds*!? Just A FEW WEEKS before!

To add to the irony, upon learning the date of our cousin Mackenzie's high school graduation, Jason and I both took time off from work and made plans to attend. Since we were going to be in Huntsville for a few days, Jason decided to make a tattoo appointment as well. (I'm sure you can already see where this story is going.) In his absence, however, I contacted the shop to keep his appointment for myself. So I could get the tattoo I recently mentioned to my technician.

Soon after confirming the appointment, I sent my tattoo artist, Adam, a copy of the picture I wanted to use for the portrait. I decided to use one of Jason's preschool pictures. Seeing this particular picture always made me smile. In the photo, Jason was wearing a green Ninja Turtles sweatshirt and a sly smile on his face. I had previously saved the picture as his contact photo in my cell phone. But since it would no longer appear there, I liked the idea of being able to glance at my forearm and see it.

The day of my appointment, Adam said he had a *potential* surprise for me. When he lifted the stencil, I noticed his "surprise" right away. He had replaced the Ninja Turtles cartoon on the front of Jason's shirt with a cartooned version of one of Erv's recent workout selfies, because he knew we often worked out together. I loved it!

The tattoo took around two hours to complete. To my surprise (and probably Adam's), I sat through the entire process without closing my eyes, squirming, balling my fists, or stopping to take a break. Erv would've been proud. Oddly enough, despite this being my largest and lengthiest piece, it was also the least painful. In addition, the tattoo came out even better than I had imagined. I couldn't have been happier.

My mom also got a tattoo that day. Her first tattoo ever, at almost 60 years old! She got Jason's name in cursive script on the inside of her wrist, with a heart coming off the letter "J." My dad later got Jason's named tattooed on him as well. His was placed at the top of his forearm with a crown above the name. This was his first tattoo as well (age 60).

It warmed my heart to see them getting tattoos honoring Erv, knowing how much he loved getting them himself. *(Erv had upwards of 20 tattoos by the time he passed away.)* I'm sure Erv was smiling proudly from Heaven on those two particular days.

In addition to the tattoos, my parents and I had other physical means of honoring Erv and his memory in the form of different paraphernalia. The first items I purchased were t-shirts. I loved the shirts my parents and I received from my cousin Kris and his wife so much that I decided to have more made. I reached out to the designer and had about 10 additional shirts printed with my favorite pictures of Erv.

Later, my mom and I had several small buttons made with some of our favorite pictures of Erv. I made (and still make) it a point to wear one every day. *(Well, unless I'm already wearing one of my t-shirts. Don't wanna overdo it, you know?)*

My mom also had two different elastic wristbands made: a silver one reading "LONG LIVE KING ERV" and a purple one reading "Jason 'J ERV' Ervin," each with the four icons used on his grave marker: a cross, a heart, a chef hat, and a microphone. Similar to the buttons, I wear a wrist band pretty much every day.

The Gym and The Music

I had always been a fan of Jason's music, but after he passed away, I became obsessed with listening to it. Simply because it was a way to hear his voice. I downloaded several additional tracks to my iPod and would listen to them often. In fact, every time I worked out, regardless of the activity, I would listen to his music and his music only, never growing tired of any of the songs.

In addition, I started incorporating the barbell bench press (Erv's favorite exercise) into my weekly workout routine. Erv had always encouraged me to use it, but I never did. I preferred to bench press with dumbbells. But in his absence, I felt compelled to bench press using the barbell instead. And every time I'd use it, I could feel his presence and hear him encouraging me.

I quickly gained strength in my chest and was lifting heavier than I ever imagined on the bench. However, after a few months of consistently bench pressing, I decided to stop. Although I loved feeling Erv's presence, I didn't like the traps, broad shoulders, and pecs I was beginning to develop.[*] When I finally decided to no longer bench press, I could hear Erv: *"Yeah, bruh. Yo a** IS gettin' a little swole"* – lol.

My Financial Blessing

As mentioned earlier, Jason started working for Sodexo as a food service manager (FSM) for the Atlanta Public Schools System in January 2017, shortly before his passing. The FSM position was full-time, salaried, and came with benefits, including a life insurance policy.

Although Jason had only been working for the company for a few months, his beneficiaries (my parents) were still eligible to receive the maximum payout on the policy, which was equal to Jason's base annual salary. The payout was divided into two checks: one for my mom and one for my dad. However, they gave half of the money to me, knowing that's what Jason would've wanted.

I remember crying at the sight of that money in my bank account. I was reminded of all the times when I had given Jason money, bought him shoes, or paid for things on his behalf, and his seemingly empty promises to repay me or return the favors by saying: *"I got you,"* or, *"It's on me next time."* It turned out those promises weren't empty after all. Not only had Erv paid me back, but he paid me several times over.

---

[*] "Traps" refer to the trapezius muscles located at the base of the neck/top of shoulders. "Pecs" is short for the pectoral (chest) muscles.

Although I would've given every penny of that money back for the opportunity to buy him another meal or another pair of Jordan's, I was beyond grateful for the blessing.

Celebration of Life

Soon after Jason passed away, I decided I wanted to host a party the following September (2017). I not only wanted to celebrate my birthday, but more importantly, I wanted to celebrate Jason's life. With the funeral being held in Huntsville, I knew many of Jason's local (Atlanta) friends and coworkers wouldn't be able to attend. So, this event would also be a means for them to pay their respects.

I wanted the event to be on a larger scale than the house parties Jason and I usually hosted. So, in addition to booking my party hostess from the year before, Kashima, I rented one of the clubhouses in my neighborhood and hired both a DJ and photographer.

The clubhouse consisted of two large adjacent rooms. I decided to use one room for the table and chairs, food, and drinks. The other room would serve as the "party room," housing the DJ and dance floor, beer pong table, and card games.

In addition to the other decorations, Kashima also suggested that we turn one wall into a photo booth for guests to take pictures, and a second wall space into a memory board where people could share their fondest memories of Jason or write a message to our family. My mom also provided buttons and wristbands for people to take home as keepsakes.

In the past, Jason and I catered the food for our events, plus or minus my mom, who would sometimes help with the desserts.

However, with Jason being a chef, people obviously assumed he prepared ALL the food, because I got asked on several occasions: *"Who's gonna make the food?"* or, *"Are you just gonna cater the food this year?"*

Now, to be completely honest, a part of me was insulted anytime anyone asked me about the food given all the hard work I always put into it, *alongside* Jason, in the past. Nonetheless, I understood their logic. So, instead of expressing my offense, I'd just answer their questions: *"Me and my mom are gonna make it,"* or, *"No, my mom and I are gonna take care of it."*

With that being said, my mom and I definitely felt the pressure to live up to Jason's (and obviously his fans') expectations of the food. So much so that planning, and later executing, the menu became a source of stress in and of itself. We desperately wanted the food to be "just right." Not only to honor Erv's culinary legacy, but also, to have a sense that he was looking down on us from the Heavens with pride.

The party was held on Saturday, September 16th – about four and a half months after Jason passed. It was scheduled from 6-11 p.m. My mom and I started prepping the food that Friday night and finished a little after 4 p.m. that Saturday. Just in time to load everything up and begin setting up the clubhouse at 5. Luckily, my cousins had come into town early, because decorating and preparing the clubhouse was an *all hands on deck* situation. I can't remember the last time I was that stressed out.

Kashima arrived at the clubhouse at 5:30 to take over for me, so I could go home and get dressed for the party. Also around that time, my friends (Alex, Erica, and Katrenia) had arrived from Huntsville and were ready and available to help. But, being the perfectionist that I am, I couldn't leave at 5:30. There was still so much work to be done. I ended up staying almost another half hour before Kashima and my friends finally kicked me out.

My cousins and I left the clubhouse and returned to my place, so I could finally get dressed for the party. Once there, however, we decided to take shots in memory of Erv. Each time we exclaimed, *"Long Live King Erv!"* We were later joined by one of my close friends and Jason's friends, Reu and Matt. And the shots continued: *"Long Live King Erv!"*

My original plan was to arrive at the party around 7, but I didn't end up getting there until after 8. When I finally made it to my room to get dressed, a dark cloud suddenly came over me. I spent most of my time in the shower crying, thinking about the "why" behind the party and the fact that Erv wouldn't be there. Once out of the shower, I had a hard time pulling myself together. For a moment, I didn't think I'd be able to attend the party at all. I was simply too emotional.

Not only were my emotions elevated, I also didn't like the way I looked in my dress. Although I had still been going to the gym on a somewhat consistent basis, my diet (or lack thereof) was terrible. I found myself eating whatever I wanted, whenever I wanted. I had begun using food for comfort versus nourishment. Consequently, I had reached an all-time high with my weight and no longer felt comfortable in my skin.

I was taking so long to get dressed that eventually my cousin Mackenzie came upstairs to check on me. Soon after she left, I pulled myself together as best I could and prepared to head back to the clubhouse. When I finally arrived, everyone in the room clapped and smiled, temporarily making me feel a little better. But my dark cloud quickly returned – not just because I was missing Jason, but also because I was disappointed in what I saw.

The decorations were perfect. However, the turnout (or lack thereof rather) was not. Even as the night went on, the turnout remained relatively low. Granted, the turnout may have appeared smaller than it was due to the size of the venue. But I was still disappointed. And honestly, what upset me most about the turnout was that some of my closest friends weren't there by the time I arrived. Many of them failed to show up all together, despite confirming their attendance earlier in the week, or even that day.

Many of Jason's friends and coworkers didn't show up for the event either, which was another disappointment. On the bright side, however, many of my coworkers and other close friends, as well as, several friends that I had not seen in years did show up for the party. I was happy to see them and thankful for their attendance.

I was also upset by the setup and presentation of the food my mom and I had worked so hard to prepare. In hindsight, the presentation was probably fine. It just wasn't laid out the way I had envisioned. And being a perfectionist, it bothered me. Nonetheless, everyone complimented me on how well the food tasted, which was the most important factor. I felt accomplished knowing my mom and I had achieved our goal of honoring Erv's culinary legacy.

Despite the positive feedback from my friends and family, overall, I was not pleased with the party. Therefore, I didn't enjoy myself as much as I had anticipated. I didn't have any additional drinks, nor did I utilize the dance floor like I had originally planned.

In fact, I spent most of the night faking smiles and fighting back tears. In the end, what was supposed to be a celebratory or happy event, put me in a state of depression, and ultimately deepened my grief.

THE REALITIES OF THE FUTURE

Chapter 10: The Acceptance

*"Sometimes your heart needs more time to accept
what your mind already knows."*
– Author Unknown

In addition to the obvious acceptance of my brother's passing, there were several other realities, or truths, that I had to accept during this time. Although each reality can easily be related to one or more others, each one was difficult to accept in and of itself. It was also my experience that trying to accept these things without becoming angry, bitter, or cold at heart presented yet another challenge.

Nonetheless, once I began to willingly accept these truths, I was able to more easily maneuver through the grieving process and ultimately begin moving forward (in the right direction) with my life.

- **Not Everyone Will Be Sympathetic Towards You and Your Situation**

This was the first additional reality I was forced to accept upon losing Jason – the fact that not everyone will have or express sympathy for you and your loss, including people you may know. This concept is initially hard to grasp because when you experience this type of loss, you immediately feel as if you are a victim. This is because, in essence – you are. And everyone is supposed to feel sorry for the victim, right?

Additionally, because your feelings and emotions are extremely heightened during this time, you're naturally in a much more sensitive state. This makes it difficult to understand how or why others are not being sensitive or sympathetic towards you and what you are a going through. In my instance: Here I am, only 32 years old, and I have just lost my brother – my one and only sibling – who was just 30 himself at the time.

Also take into consideration, we have lived under the same roof most of our lives, and for the last 4-plus years, he has lived under my roof in Atlanta. Away from our parents and with no other family in the city. Thus, leaving me "alone" in more ways than one. I can recall thinking: *"How could you NOT feel sorry for me!?"*

I would imagine a stranger would feel a sense of pity for someone in my situation. I would, if the roles were reversed. So, imagine how hard it is to accept or understand someone you know personally or whom you deal with on a regular basis *not* showing you the sympathy you feel you rightfully deserve. In my case, this was my immediate supervisor at work.

As previously mentioned, during my initial time off, I set up a meeting with the pharmacy supervisor and the district manager to discuss the need to reduce my hours at work upon Jason's passing. They both were very sympathetic during the meeting and easily agreed to the reduction. However, soon after I returned to work (after just 6 short weeks), the sympathy I thought my supervisor had for me and my situation seemed nonexistent. In fact, he eventually become downright rude and inconsiderate.

The first incident was about two months after I returned to work and occurred during my first scheduled vacation, which was originally to be used for our annual cruise. It is important to note, this was my first family vacation in 30 years without Jason, so one can only imagine how emotional it was. As a result, I spent much of my "vacation" grieving with my parents.

I was scheduled to be off from work for almost a week. On my second day off, a Wednesday, my supervisor contacted me via text message about a non-urgent work-related issue. I informed him that I was out on vacation with my parents and that I would handle the issue upon my return to work the following week. He responded saying he was unaware of my time off, so I didn't hold the interruption against him.

However, that Friday, I received a second message from him (also of a non-urgent nature) and then yet again that Monday morning! At that point, I felt blatantly disrespected. I went from being slightly annoyed to being furious. So much so, that I decided to share my feelings with him.

Normally, I would've scheduled a meeting with him to address my concerns, but this couldn't wait. I sent him a text message detailing the events that had recently occurred and how it made me feel given the circumstances. I also reminded him that on his very first conference call with our district (because he was still relatively new at the time), he had asked a favor of us:

If he is out on vacation and an issue arises that can be handled upon his return (in other words, if the issue isn't urgent), he would appreciate it, if we would wait until his return to address the matter. Can you believe that!? He asked that favor of his team, then had the audacity to bother, or pretty much harass, me during my vacation (or time of grief, rather).

Now, I must admit, he was very apologetic for his actions, and just like in my initial meeting with him and the district manager, he seemed to be sympathetic of my situation. However, just like before, I quickly realized that was not the case.

I won't go into any other specific instances or details (and there were several). But I will say, although he never came out and verbally said: *"I know your brother passed away, but you should be over that by now"* or *"but your work shouldn't be affected at this point,"* his actions (or lack thereof) implied exactly that.

At this point, I began to question myself: *"Is he right? It's been a few months now, should I be 'over it'? Should I be functioning normally at this point?"* After all, I had never been through anything like this. I didn't know what was considered a "normal" grieving period.

The answer to my questions: *"No. No. And no."* In fact, I will NEVER be "over it" – ever. And the sad truth is, the "normal" grieving period is for a lifetime. It is eternal. I believe as more and more time passes, one is better able to manage his or her expressions of grief, but the grief itself never goes away. So, the hope or prayer is that with time, you are better able to function and maintain a somewhat normal way of life.

As for my supervisor, I eventually accepted the fact that I would not receive any sympathy from him and stopped expecting it. This was hard to do at first, considering I had to interact with him on a weekly basis, but once I managed to do so, it made doing my job a lot less stressful.

I remember my mom saying she constantly prayed for his heart to change, for him to become more sympathetic. I, on the other hand, never prayed for my supervisor to change. I only prayed for myself – for the strength and guidance to handle working with him during this difficult time.

The reason I never prayed for my supervisor was simple: I believe the only way a person like him – someone who is unsympathetic by nature – will potentially become more sympathetic to someone in a situation like mine, is to experience some sort of tragedy or loss of his (or her) own. And I wouldn't wish that on my worst enemy.

- **People You Assumed You Could Depend On, May Disappoint You**

Similar to the aforementioned reality, this truth is also hard to accept because you now have a victim's mentality. So, in your mind, if a person is close to you (the victim), such as a friend or relative, then the assumption is that during your time of need, you should be able to depend on this person.

Just like in other times of crisis, the people dearest or closest to the victim, are often (or at least should be) the first to offer their love, support, and assistance to the victim and their family. Unfortunately, I had to come to the realization that this wasn't always the case.

There are two specific instances in which I can vividly recall being disappointed by some of the people closest to me. The first instance was around the time of Jason's funeral. With the funeral being held during the week and in Huntsville versus Atlanta, I didn't expect many of the people Jason and I had developed friendships or relationships with to attend.

To be honest, outside of our family, the only people I specifically expected to be in attendance, were the people who made it a point to tell me they would be there. With that being said, a particular friend comes to mind: Sonya.*

Sonya and I had known each other and been friends for about 10 years at the time of Jason's passing. Not only did she have a relationship with me, she also knew Jason and had become fond of him as well. To put our friendship into perspective, if I were planning my wedding, I would've asked Sonya to be a bridesmaid. So, we were close.

That being the case, when she confirmed she'd be at the funeral, I expected her to be there. In fact, she had taken it a step further by saying she'd be in town the day before in case I needed help with anything. So, imagine how disappointed and hurt I felt when she not only neglected to show up for the funeral, but also made no attempt to contact me in the weeks and months to follow. To date (six months since the funeral), I still have not had a phone conversation with Sonya.

The second instance was surrounding the party I hosted to celebrate my birthday and Jason's life. I invited a number of our friends and acquaintances to attend, and although I knew some of my closest friends wouldn't be able to make it due to prior engagements and responsibilities, I still expected certain people to be in attendance.

Similar to the funeral scenario, I not only expected people to be there because of our friendship or relationship, but also because they explicitly said they would be. However, several of the people closest

---

* Name has been changed.

to me (and Jason) didn't show up for the party. Some of them didn't even bother to reach out after the event, an additional hard pill to swallow.

These incidents may seem similar. However, I want to explain how they differ. Although I would have appreciated knowing Sonya was present at Jason's funeral, it was in the weeks and months to come *after* the funeral when I needed her most. When the additional phone calls, visits, and acts of sympathy from other people began to slow down.

Conversely, I needed the most support from friends and loved ones *during* my party. I was an emotional wreck by the time of the event. So, having certain people there, especially those people who had been supporting me with their presence since the funeral, would have been greatly appreciated and likely helpful in easing some of my emotional stress.

Let me be the first to mention, however, I understand that my friends and loved ones in both instances probably had good intentions. More than likely, they originally planned to attend the respective events. I also understand situations may have come up in their lives, or their circumstances may have changed in such a way, that no longer rendered them able to attend. Believe me, given the current events in my life at the time, I wholeheartedly empathize with those probabilities and possibilities.

But to be truthful, being able to understand or grasp those concepts doesn't make the incidents any less hurtful, especially when no additional contact was attempted after the original disappointment. Yet and still, I am thankful for my friends and loved ones who showed their love and support by attending the funeral and my party after

Jason's passing. Additionally, I appreciate those who made an effort to reach out (and have continued to reach out) after the respective events.

In the end, however, I had to realize that it was my own expectations that caused me to be disappointed in both instances. Were my expectations reasonable given the circumstances? Yes, of course they were. But as the saying goes, *"If you depend on others for your happiness, you will often be disappointed."* Even if those "others" are those nearest and dearest to you.

- **Your Friendships Might Change – And Not Always for the Better**

No one wants to lose someone they considered to be a friend, especially during a time of grief, when you need your friends the most. In fact, you'd like to think that your friendships and relationships with the people you care about would strengthen during this difficult time. It was my experience, however, that some of the people I considered to be my close friends distanced themselves from me after I lost Jason. Thus altering, or in some cases, permanently damaging, the friendship we once had.

What makes this such a hard reality to accept is the lack of closure. Not knowing exactly why your friend (or friends) decided to become distant during such a difficult time in your life:

"Was it because they didn't know what to say, so they decided to say nothing at all? Do they feel guilty about their initial reaction or distance and are now too embarrassed to reach out, due to how much time has passed or what they think you might say? Was it that they

simply couldn't bear the thought of seeing or talking to you knowing you've experienced such a tragic loss? Or, given their relationship with your loved one, perhaps they too are having a difficult time coping with the loss?"

Although this list could probably go on, I assume these are some of the more common explanations or reasons. However, regardless of the reasoning, the distance is hurtful. And quite frankly, any reason other than a concurrent tragic or unexpected event of their own, just seems selfish to the person experiencing the loss.

If you don't know what to say, then say exactly that. For example, *"I don't know what to say, but I just want you to know I'm here for you."* Because honestly, there's nothing anyone can say that will be of much consolation to the person coping with the loss. However, simply making yourself available to that person will be greatly appreciated in the event they need your love, care, and support during that time.

On the other hand, choosing to say nothing at all, is probably the worst thing you can do. During a person's time of grief, they need (and want) to know they're in the thoughts and prayers of the people they consider to be their friends.

If it's been several weeks, or even months, since you've contacted your friend, or if you haven't reached out at all since the initial notification of their loss, reach out anyway! Even if your friend was initially disappointed by your distance, if the two of you are or were truly friends, chances are that person will still be glad to hear from you. Remember *true* bonds don't break. They may bend, but they don't break.

If you hate the thought of seeing or talking to your friend during such a rough period in their life, imagine how much harder it must be for them, feeling as though they can't rely on one of their close friends to help them get through it. After all, being a good friend means being there to love and support your friend not only during their good days, but also (and probably more importantly) during their bad ones.

The last scenario mentioned, actually occurred when I finally asked one of my good friends why he hadn't made himself available to support me (as much as I would've expected him to) upon Jason's passing, especially considering he had a relationship with both of us. He informed me that Jason's passing was his first experience with death, as he had never lost any family members or friends. So, he himself, was having a hard time coping with the loss.

This was understandable, but still selfish, nonetheless. I say this because, although he was concurrently grieving the loss, the truth of the matter is, his grief would only last for a season. At some point, he would get over the fact that Jason passed away and go on with his life as if nothing ever happened. Conversely, my grief will last for a lifetime.

Ergo (as I expressed to him), I felt as though he still should have made the effort to support me during my time of need, even if that meant temporarily putting his own feelings aside. Unfortunately, he didn't necessarily agree, and our friendship was never quite the same.

Be that as it may, I am grateful for the people and friends who never stopped showing (and even increased) their love and support during my time of need. I am also thankful for the new friendships and relationships that have developed during this process. Furthermore, regardless of the reason behind the distance or the amount of time that has lapsed, I am always open to the possibility of mending friendships and reuniting with old friends.

- **You Must Make Every Effort to Protect Your Heart**

When Jason passed away, my heart was instantly broken into a thousand unrepairable pieces, leaving me in what felt like a permanent state of fragility. In addition, I became extremely sensitive due to my heightened emotional state. Hence, it became of dire importance that I take whatever actions I deemed necessary to protect my damaged heart and, ultimately, my sanity.

The best example of this was the *"everyone is dispensable"* mentality I developed during my initial grieving period. Upon losing Jason, who was not only my brother, but also my best friend, in my mind, there wasn't a person left in this world I couldn't (and wouldn't be willing to) live without. Outside of my parents, I made no exceptions. I was in a place where peace of mind was my number one priority.

That being the case, if someone – whether it be a friend, family member, acquaintance, or otherwise – threatened my peace, my current goals, or my potential happiness, then that person had to go. It was just that simple. I considered them a *"casualty of my grief."* Was this decision always easy? No. But, was it necessary? Absolutely.

Being that I was emotionally drained during this time, protecting my energy was also of utmost importance. I no longer spent energy entertaining meaningless friendships or relationships, forcing interactions, engaging in unnecessary conversations, or making myself available to people who seemed unavailable to me. I simply could not and would not do it. I only had enough energy to take care of myself each individual day, and even that was a struggle at times.

Choosing to accept all the previously mentioned realties, or truths, was also a means of protecting my fragmented heart and limited energy. Albeit none of them were easy to accept in the beginning, just like my *"everyone is dispensable"* mentality, their acceptance was necessary.

This is not to say that, during that time, I didn't care about any of my impaired friendships or relationships, the casualties of my grief, or those affected by my energy shift. I simply cared about myself more. I was in survival mode. And since you need your heart to survive, I was determined to protect what was left of mine.

- **Life Goes On**

This was the final and probably hardest reality I had to accept: That despite my loss, and all the heartache and grief surrounding it, that life simply goes on. Meaning, although life as I knew it had ended, life in and of itself continued. I realized this to a small extent immediately after the funeral when the additional phone calls, visits, and acts of sympathy became fewer and farther in between. But it wasn't until later in the grieving process that I accepted this reality as a fact.

This was initially hard to accept because after losing Jason, nothing in or about my life seemed to be the same. Ultimately, I knew it never would be. I felt as if I had two lives: My first life beginning

September 12,1984 and ending with the loss of my brother on April 29, 2017. My second life began April 30th of that year. The first full day I had to live without him.

During my initial grieving period, I came across a poem who's ending perfectly summed up the way I felt:

It broke my heart to lose you,
But you didn't go alone.
Part of me went with you,
The day God called you home.[*]

Feeling this way, it was often difficult to see the people I knew moving on with their lives per usual. But I had to accept it, because this was a part of my new reality, or my new life.

For example, something as simple as noticing a friend has posted a picture on Facebook or Instagram with his or her sibling, or better yet their brother, knowing that I can no longer create memories or post current pictures with mine, was devastating. But if I chose to remain active on social media, what could I do about it? Nothing. As hard as it was, I simply had to accept it – because life goes on.

Soon after the funeral, the acts of sympathy from people other than your close friends and loved ones begin to slow down. However, over time, you realize your close friends' and loved ones' acts of sympathy become fewer and farther in between as well. But because you still feel victimized at this point, at times, it's hard to accept that you are no longer receiving the attention or help you once did – especially from those that are nearest and dearest to you.

[*] The poem was entitled, *The Day God Called You Home.*

This is not to say that you are no longer in the thoughts and prayers of your friends and loved ones, because more than likely you are. You must be mindful of the fact, however, that your friends and loved ones have things, circumstances, and situations in their own lives to take care of, handle, or cope with. They too may be "victims" in a sense. Still, rest assured in the event that you need your friends or loved ones during this difficult time, they will make every effort to be there for you.

Having said that, the fact that life does indeed continue, is also the most promising reality to accept. Continued life (or as I refer to it, new life) also comes with new opportunities. And despite not knowing how you will find the strength or the exact date and time in which it will occur, the truth of the matter is, you *will* learn to live again.

Yet being completely transparent as the author, as I am writing this exert, I am unaware of how or when I will truly begin to "live" again myself. However, I am prayerful and confident that one day I will.

Chapter 11: The Cocoon

> *"Come quickly, Lord, and answer me,*
> *for my depression deepens…"*
> (Psalms 143:7[*])

You may or may not have noticed, but in the previous chapter I mentioned my *initial* grieving period. This is because, immediately after my birthday, or celebration of [Erv's] life event, I went into a second, or what I refer to as a *real* or *deep* grieving period.

This was a very dark time for me. I initially (for at least two weeks) ceased ALL communication with any- and everyone other than my parents and colleagues from work. I neglected to answer or return any phone calls. I failed to read or reply to any text messages. And I stopped being active and making posts on my social media accounts.

I was in a grave state of depression. The only tasks I completed were those I deemed imperative: eating, sleeping, working, and working out. And even those things were a struggle. I also cried and prayed (often at the same time) more during those two weeks than I had since the hospital and funeral. I was not only in a state of helplessness, but also hopelessness.

I easily lost ten pounds during the first two weeks of my depression, as my appetite was often nonexistent. My sleep pattern was erratic. Some nights I slept, some nights I didn't. This left me

[*] From the New Living Translation (NLT).

tired and sluggish. I managed to make it to work each day that I was scheduled, but my ability to perform at a high level became more and more difficult.

Even though my workouts were consistent, each one was a forced effort. I didn't want to go the gym. Hell, I didn't want to go anywhere. And on top of all that, I was an emotional wreck, often crying uncontrollably, yelling out to God and my angel for help.

There were several factors or circumstances that led me to that point – to that *real* or *deep* grieving period. The first factor was my inability to truly grieve in the beginning. Although I took six weeks off from work when Jason passed away, I didn't have much time (if any) to myself during that period.

During that time, I was always preoccupied with something else: making funeral arrangements, spending time in Alabama with my parents, entertaining visitors and other family members, etc. So, I never really had any time alone to cope with my loss. And by the time things began to slow down, it was time for me to return to work.

Returning to work was onerous in and of itself. Although the distraction seemed to be a good thing at times, the additional stress it created often was not. I was also having a difficult time separating my grief from my practice, which over time, hindered my ability to perform at a consistently acceptable level. In addition, having a supervisor who was unsympathetic to my circumstances, made an already arduous situation that much harder. As a result, my job not only became an additional source of stress, but also an additional source of grief.

Soon after returning to work, I began making preparations for the party I was hosting in September. Preparing for the party also hindered my ability to just "stop" and take the time necessary to truly grieve the loss of my brother.

Considering I had put so much pressure on myself to have everything as close to perfect for the party as possible, the preparations occupied *a lot* of my thoughts and free time. And just like my job, what originally seemed like a good distraction (even more so because it pertained to Erv), ultimately ended up being a huge source of stress.

In hindsight, I realize in the time leading up to the party, I tried my hardest to remain strong knowing the event was ahead. I never wanted to feel like "it" – the grief, my job, the party preparations, etc. – was too much. No matter what, I wanted to stay strong enough to host that party, because it meant so much to me. I wanted to honor Erv, and I was determined to do so.

The party, however, ultimately ended up being a harrowing experience for me. I was emotionally distraught beforehand. And overall, I was disappointed with the turnout, especially the absence of my and Erv's closest friends and loved ones. Plus, the lack of reconciliation by many of these friends and loved ones, made an already disappointing situation even more hurtful.

To make matters worse, almost immediately after the party, the situation with my supervisor escalated. And with the party and associated preparations finally being over, I no longer had any distractions to occupy my thoughts and free time. Hence, my grief was finally able to *truly* settle in. It was the realization, acceptance, and accumulation of all these things that ultimately put me in that dark place: my cocoon.

My *cocoon phase*, or temporary separation from the outside world, lasted for months. Although I reopened the lines of communication with some of my friends and loved ones after those initial two weeks, I remained inactive on social media and refused to take part in any social outings or functions. I wanted to be alone, so I kept to myself. Besides work, the gym, or to get food (grocery store, pizza place, etc.), I didn't go much of anywhere.

I take that back. I still went to the nail shop regularly. To be honest, I made it a point to go. Although I was going through what felt like Hell on Earth, I never wanted to *look* like what I was going through. I made a conscious effort to keep my hair and nails done, feet pedicured, and eyebrows waxed. Even though I no longer felt strong on the inside, it was important to me that I appeared confident and strong on the outside.

It was also during my cocoon phase that I decided to write this book. I had never written a book before and had no idea where to start. All I knew was, I had a story to tell. So, I got a notebook and began writing any- and everything that came to mind. I carried my notebook everywhere. And anytime a thought, memory, or idea crossed my mind, I made a point to write it down – right then and there.

My only exception was when I was working. I didn't take my notebook to the pharmacy because I was already having a difficult time focusing when I was there. However, if something associated with the book happened to cross my mind during one of my shifts, I'd make a note of it in my phone and transfer it to my notebook when I got home.

Soon after I begun journaling ideas for the book, I purchased a laptop and began putting my notes into a readable format. During this time, I still made use of my notebook as well, jotting down any additional thoughts or memories as they came to mind.

It wasn't long before I became obsessed. I'd wake up early and stay up late in an effort to add a few extra pages. I'd carry my laptop to the nail shop, pizza place, or anywhere else I thought I might have some time to write. Long story short, I wasn't an author (yet), but I was writing!

Attempting to write this book proved to be a worthwhile experience during my cocoon phase for several reasons. The first reason simply being, it gave me something to do. It was something to occupy my time (and thoughts) outside of work and the gym. Secondly, writing was almost therapeutic for me. It was a means to share and express my memories, thoughts, feelings, and experiences without any judgment, questions, or rebuttal.

Finally, writing this book gave me another way to honor Erv and his memory. Although I didn't know how or when I would have the book published, I knew I would. I was determined to share my story – for myself, but more so for Erv. In hindsight, this explains my obsession. Upon Erv's passing, I became obsessed with any- and everything associated with him and his memory.

There were three definitive moments or experiences, two positive and one negative, that occurred during my cocoon phase and ultimately assisted in my progression to the next level or chapter in my life. I am thankful the positive experiences occurred first, because they, in part, gave me the strength and courage necessary to endure the third, or negative, experience.

In fact, after the negative moment occurred, I revisited the positive experiences and received even more motivation, clarity, and insight than I had originally. For that reason (and because I prefer to end my narrative on a high note), I will discuss the negative experience here and elaborate on the positive experiences in the next chapter.

"Coach and Counsel"

At my company, when an employee's performance is less than stellar, he or she runs the risk of receiving what is referred to as a "coach and counsel," which is a nice way of saying *a write-up*. This process occurs in four steps, or levels.

Upon one's first offense (level 1), he or she might receive a written warning or "coaching" about their behavior versus the expected or required behavior. Subsequent offenses of the same nature can result in additional write-ups or "counseling" – level 2 or level 3 depending on the number of previous offenses. However, certain behaviors (or lack thereof) can result in an instant level 2 counseling. Finally, a fourth (or level 4) counseling can be grounds for termination.

When I returned to work, I stayed in the pharmacy manager role. However, soon after returning, I realized the additional responsibilities associated with being manager were overwhelming given my current mental and emotional state.

So, when the time came for pharmacy managers to meet individually with the pharmacy supervisor for our annual reviews (a couple months after my return), I discussed my concerns with my supervisor. I asked to step down from my management position, even if it were only temporary, as the job was currently too much for me to take on, resulting in my subpar performance. Due to my loss, I simply did not have the energy to perform my job the way I once had or to the level that was expected.

My supervisor informed me that he did not have any lower level (staff pharmacist) positions available in his district at the time. I understood and offered a second (and possibly easier) solution: My partner (staff pharmacist) and I could temporarily switch roles until I was in better position to resume my management role.[*]

Unfortunately, my supervisor was not receptive to this idea. Instead, he suggested that I take another leave of absence (LOA). But considering I had recently returned from a 6-week unpaid LOA, I wasn't in the best financial position to take another one. Consequently, I had to remain in my management position.

As it got nearer to my and Jason's birthday and the celebratory party I had been planning, I began to feel worse and worse emotionally. I could feel my strength weakening and my anxiety creeping back into my life after being absent for so many years. So, separating what I was going through from my job became even more challenging.

As to be expected, my performance not only failed to improve, but began to decline even further. As much as I loved my job, and more importantly, as much as I *needed* my job, I couldn't seem to muster up the mental strength (and to be completely honest, the care or concern) to push myself to a higher level of performance. I wanted to,

---

[*] Most public retail pharmacies (other than those with extended hours or 24-hour operation) have two pharmacists – a pharmacy manager and a staff pharmacist – who alternate or rotate shifts to cover the pharmacy's operating hours throughout the week.

but I just couldn't. In the end, all I cared about was the loss of my brother and finding a way to get through this grievous period.

It didn't take long for my supervisor to notice the steady decline in my performance as well. Soon after I returned from vacation in September (in celebration of my and Jason's birthdays), he asked his administrative assistant to schedule a meeting with me. Although I didn't know the specific details of the meeting, given my current performance and how everything was going (or not going, rather) at my store in combination with my supervisor's unsympathetic attitude, I was sure of one thing: The upcoming meeting would *not* be a good one.

The meeting with my supervisor was held on Friday, October 6, 2017. Ironically, this was one day after I wrote the previous exert about him (*Chapter 10: The Acceptance*). And although I knew the meeting probably wouldn't go (or at least end) well, I never imagined it would go the way it did.

The meeting started off okay, with my supervisor initially asking for my thoughts on the current state of the pharmacy (in terms of the company metrics) and a possible plan of action for the identified deficiencies, as we were now considered a "challenged pharmacy." I addressed the overall poor state of the pharmacy; the progress or "small wins" we had made and accomplished thus far; and a general plan for ways to improve each individual metric.

My supervisor then switched gears for a moment to discuss the results of a recent loss prevention (LP) audit that had taken place at my store before returning to the metrics discussion. Although the pharmacy passed the LP audit, because we passed with an 84 instead of 85%, being pharmacy manager, I received an automatic level 2 counsel (write-up) – which I didn't dispute. It wasn't until he returned to the previous discussion that the meeting took a turn for the worst.

My supervisor ultimately agreed with the things I had said about the current state of the pharmacy. He also appeared to like and agree with most of my plans or ideas for improvement. His major concern, however, was not how but *when* the situation in the pharmacy would finally turn around and the metrics would be at (or at least near) target. I couldn't give him an exact date or even a potential timeline because I didn't know myself.

I then explained how I was still struggling at work due to the loss of my brother, in fact, even more so than before. I also again suggested that it was in my best interest, not to mention the store's, if I step down from my pharmacy management position. Even with the slight reduction in my hours, I simply did not have the extra energy to perform the pharmacy manager role at the level necessary to turn the metrics around. At least not at that moment in time and certainly not at the speed in which my supervisor was expecting.

Similar to our previous meeting, my supervisor informed me that there were no staff pharmacist positions available in the district. So, stepping down was still not an option at the time. He then suggested three temporary solutions or alternatives: 1) that I take some additional time off (another leave of absence); 2) that I contact the employee assistance program (EAP) for help coping with my situation; or 3) that he would assist in my possible transfer to another district.

I responded that I was still not in the best financial position to take another unpaid leave – so that was out. I also had no desire to call the EAP line. Albeit, I didn't know what type of "assistance" they offered employees, I simply wasn't interested in contacting them.

Even though transferring to a neighboring district sounded like a plausible suggestion, the thought of my supervisor shopping me around to other supervisors, as if I were damaged goods, didn't sit well with me. Although I was going through a rough patch, I knew my value and worth as a pharmacist. So, I declined that option as well.

My supervisor became frustrated at this point. The pharmacy was in a "challenged" state. I, as manager, didn't seem to care about restoring it (in his opinion). And I wasn't open to any of the possible solutions he had offered. Then, what I considered to be the unthinkable happened.

My supervisor said: *"I understand you've been through a lot, but everybody's going through something"* – obviously implying my situation was no heavier or any different from the next person's. He continued: *"So my expectation is that when you come through those doors to work, you forget about any- and everything else you may be going through…and do your job."*

He then proceeded to hand me a second level 2 counseling, this time for my performance, or lack thereof, I guess. (Let me remind you: This was, ironically, the VERY NEXT DAY after I had *just* written or mentioned the fact that he had never verbalized, what I knew, he had been feeling or thinking the entire time. The very next day!)

I mentally checked out and completely shut down at that point. As far I was concerned, the meeting was over. I remember just sitting there, facing the wall with tears in my eyes, while he continued with the meeting in my periphery, discussing the details of the second write-up.

It is important to note, however, the tears in my eyes did not occur due to my feelings being hurt. For that to be the case, it would've required that I cared about my supervisor or the relationship that we had. And I didn't give a damn about him. We had no relationship. He didn't know me, which was part of the reason he was able (and obviously thought it was okay) to talk to and treat me the way he did. So, those tears were unequivocally no manifestation of me being hurt by him in any way. Let's be clear.

My tears were associated with two different emotions, the first one being rage. Although I knew all along my supervisor felt that way, I was livid that he had the audacity to say it to my face, *especially* considering it hadn't even been six months since Jason had passed and my family laid his body to rest.

Not to mention, with the holidays being right around the corner, I still had several tough days and hard times ahead of me that year. This would be the first Thanksgiving and the first Christmas I've had in 30 years (so in essence, the first I can remember) without my brother. And the following year, I'd have to deal or cope with the first anniversary of his passing.

The second emotion was grief. Not necessarily because of the obvious fact that Jason had passed away. But more so, because I had just gotten upset about something work-related, and I couldn't call Erv afterwards to vent about it. Or at least, vent when he or I finally made it home, like I would've done under normal circumstances. Because that's what we always did. When one of us had a problem or issue at work, we'd vent to the other person.

Nonetheless, returning to the story at hand: The meeting with my supervisor ended soon after that incident. I'm not sure if he was truly finished with the meeting or if he realized and accepted the fact that I was no longer engaged in the conversation, but it ended.

I signed the second counseling, thus, agreeing to whatever it was he had written and discussed, then left his office. I left that building not knowing what I was going to do next. All I knew was, I would eventually have to do something.

My mom was the first person I called upon arriving to my car. She knew about the scheduled meeting and was eagerly awaiting the details of how it went. As to be expected, she was saddened when she learned what I had endured. She also understood and expressed, however, if things at the pharmacy didn't improve, eventually my job could be at risk. She then asked what I was going to do, because losing my job obviously was not an option.

I agreed, knowing if I lost my job, I'd lose everything. She responded: *"And you know Jason wouldn't want you to lose everything. I know you already feel like you have [in losing him], but he wouldn't want you to lose everything you've worked so hard for."* I responded: *"Yeah, you're right. But I also know, he wouldn't want me taking this sh*t from [my supervisor] either!"*

In that moment, I could hear Erv saying: *"Yeah bruh, you gotta do something. 'Cause he got you f***ed up!"* Talking to me roughly, like he always did. But after hearing his voice, it was as if something clicked. I knew it was time to begin dusting myself off and coming up with a concise plan of action. Not only pertaining to my job, but also pertaining to my "new life" in general.

After venting to my mom and some other friends about the incident with my supervisor, I took the time to simply be still and pray. I asked God for guidance and discernment, even if it were only a short-term or temporary solution. It wasn't long before my prayers were answered.

Even though I wasn't in the best financial position to take another unpaid leave of absence (LOA) from work, I remembered a conversation I had with a human resources (HR) representative during my initial LOA. She informed me that although my current leave was unpaid, if at any point – then or in the future – my doctor deemed it medically necessary for me to be away from work due to my loss, that I would qualify for a medical leave.

Taking a medical leave would then qualify me for payment via short-term disability. I can remember crying and thanking God for reminding me of that possibility. If approved, it meant I could not only take the additional time away from work I so desperately needed, but also be paid a portion of my salary!

On the Monday following the meeting, I called my doctor's office to schedule an appointment. Luckily, there was an opening the very next day. I also attempted to contact HR, but since the office was closed for the Columbus Day holiday, I had to wait until Tuesday morning to discuss the details of taking a medical leave.

To my surprise, it was a very simple process. Essentially, I could be off from work for as long as my physician deemed medically necessary. On top of that, my LOA could begin as early as the next day if my doctor saw fit.

That afternoon I met with my doctor to discuss what I had been going through and my need to take a medical leave from work. He saw fit for me to be off for a period of at least one month beginning right away. However, I asked if the leave could begin the following Monday instead. I wanted to tie up some loose ends at work. More importantly, I wanted to tell my team in person that I would be out for at least the next month.

Later that afternoon I notified my supervisor with this text message:

> *Over the weekend I took time to think about our meeting. I decided to take your suggestion about taking some additional time off. I agree that I need more time away from work to cope with my loss. Since HR was closed due to the holiday yesterday, I contacted them this morning. I also visited my doctor this afternoon. As a result, I will be on medical leave for at least a month beginning this coming Monday, the 16th. Thanks.*

It felt so good sending my supervisor that text, knowing that God had not only worked the situation out in my favor, but He had worked it out so quickly. Since I was already scheduled to be off that upcoming weekend (Friday through Sunday), my last day at work was the Thursday prior to my leave date. This meant that within a week after meeting with my supervisor, I was out on leave.

Considering it took my supervisor several hours to respond to my text, I'm pretty sure he was angry. Not necessarily that I was taking a leave, but more so because I didn't give him what he probably felt was an adequate heads-up. He was selfish like that. But if he were to be mad at anyone, it should be himself. After all, I was just taking his advice, right?

Chapter 12: The Butterfly

"I know the plans I have in mind for you,
declares the Lord; they are plans for peace, not disaster,
to give you a future filled with hope."
(Jeremiah 29:11[*])

As mentioned in the last chapter, there were three definitive moments or experiences – two positive and one negative – that occurred during my cocoon phase, which ultimately assisted in my progression to the next level or chapter in my life. Despite the positive experiences occurring before the negative one, I chose to wait and discuss the positive moments here, since I visited both experiences for a second time after the incident with my supervisor. Subsequently, I was able to gain more motivation, clarity, and insight than I had originally.

A Message from Pastor Curney: "You Don't Know My Story"

After the initial two weeks of my cocoon phase, my mom decided to come visit me in Atlanta for a few days. She came in town on a Saturday and suggested that we go to church (New Mercies) the following morning. I am so thankful I agreed. I remember feeling as if the entire church service was just for me: the music ministry, the

[*] Common English Bible (CEB).

spoken prayers, the communion, and especially Pastor Curney's sermon.

Several of the key points Pastor Curney pulled from his interpretation of the scripture touched me in such a way, that I instantly gained clarity on many of the situations and circumstances I was dealing with surrounding the passing of my brother. Thus, restoring my faith in God and His limitless abilities.

In addition, hearing his sermon prior to the incident with my supervisor, allowed me to endure (and not be broken by) the events that ensued during the meeting. Although I didn't know how, I had faith and was confident that God was going to work the situation out for my benefit.

Scripture Interpretation

Pastor's Curney's message was based on 2nd Samuel, Chapter 6. A story about the Ark of the Covenant being brought to Jerusalem by King David.* The story begins with a description of how David initially set out to bring the Ark from Judah. He gathered thousands of men to assist him, but the Ark was guided by two of his closest men, Uzzah and Ahio.

As they were traveling, they hit a bump in the road. In an effort to protect the Ark from falling, Uzzah reached out and grabbed it. But touching the Ark was an irreverent act in the eyes of the Lord. Consequently, the Lord's anger burned Uzzah, killing him on the spot.

---

* The Ark of the Covenant represented God or God's presence.

David became angry with the Lord for killing Uzzah. He also became afraid of the Lord and was no longer willing to take the Ark into Jerusalem with him. Instead, he took the Ark to a friend's house and left it there for three months.

With the Ark stationed at his friend's home, the Lord blessed his friend's entire household. When word got back to David that the Lord had blessed his friend's household due to the presence of the Ark, David went to retrieve it. He then joyfully continued with his original plans of bringing the Ark to Jerusalem.

While heading to Jerusalem, David made sacrifices unto the Lord and danced before the Him with all his might. As David and the Ark were entering the city, David's wife, Michal, watched from a window. When she saw David dancing unto the Lord, she became bitter, despising him in her heart.

When David returned home, he was confronted by Michal. She criticized him for dancing and baring himself in front of the "slave girls of his servants," in a way that appeared vulgar in her eyes. David replied to Michal, saying that he was dancing before the Lord, praising God for appointing him to rule over the Lord's people.

David then said he will continue to praise the Lord. Thus, becoming even more undignified than she had just witnessed. And although he may be humiliated in his own [and her] eyes, he would be held in honor by the slave girls whom she had mentioned.

- **"You Have a Purpose"**

Just like David's divine purpose was to rule over the Lord's people and to transport the Ark of the Covenant from Judah to Jerusalem,

Pastor Curney reminded us that, we too, have a purpose. And despite our flaws or issues, God created us to do "exceptional work." He also noted the evidence that we do indeed or *still* have a purpose, is the fact that we are still here.

Although hard to accept, this helped me understand that in the span of 30 years, Jason served his purpose here on Earth. This was made even more evident by the amount of love and feedback my family received upon his passing. Despite his flaws, Jason had impacted so many people's lives, in so many different ways – both male and female, all ages, all races, and regardless of sexual orientation, social status, or how long the person may have known him.

In almost all cases, to know Jason – via his culinary career, his music, or simply his personality – was to love Jason. And to think and know, that MY little brother, was special enough, to not only leave that big of an impression on so many people, but to also serve his purpose here on Earth – his *divine* purpose – in 30 short years, ultimately makes me proud.

- **"Things (and People) of God Must Be Handled a Certain Way"**

Although in essence, Uzzah was attempting to do a good thing by reaching out and grabbing the Ark in an effort to keep it from falling, Pastor Curney reminded us that when it comes to the things (and people) of God, *"you can't handle them any kind of way."* And doing the opposite will often result in consequences and repercussions. In this case, Uzzah being killed on the spot.

Pastor Curney also encouraged us to know, believe, and assert: *"You can't handle me any kind of way when I belong to the Lord."* This means we shouldn't worry about what certain people have said or done to us (in other words, how they've handled us), because *"God will handle people when they mishandle you."*

When I listened to the sermon for the second time, I instantly thought about my supervisor. After all, he *definitely* mishandled me in our meeting. But I could rest assured, because I knew and believed God would handle him in His own time. And although I didn't know how the situation would play out in the end, I had faith and was confident God was going to work it out in my favor.

- **"There Is 'Rock Bottom' In My Story"**

David hit rock bottom in this chapter. Pastor Curney said this was evident because after Uzzah was killed, David became angry and afraid of the Lord. So much so, that he left the Ark (God's presence) for 90 days.

According to Pastor Curney, this was the wrong action to take. When David was (or when we are) angry or afraid of God, that is not the time to draw away from Him. Instead, we as believers should draw closer to Him in order to get the help – clarity, understanding, peace, or love – that we need.

I hit rock bottom when Jason passed away. Although I wasn't necessarily afraid of God, I was certainly upset with and disappointed in Him. At times I even found myself angry with Him. I simply couldn't understand why He allowed such a tragic event to occur in my life, especially at such a young age.

Like David, I distanced myself from God. I had no desire to go to church, and my prayers got fewer and farther in between. It got to the point where I didn't want anyone to mention God or prayer to me. I just told people to pray for me, because I was *"all prayed out."*

In hindsight, in the months following the funeral, as my prayers became fewer and farther in between, my grief got heavier. And my ability to cope with my loss on my own seemed to gradually diminish. It was only when I started back praying and asking God for help (during my cocoon phase) that I began to feel any better. Additionally, returning to church and having my faith in God fully restored has given me the strength and confidence to know that I will not only get through this, but I will continue to thrive as a result.

- **"There Is Joy About the Will of God in My Story"**

Pastor Curney noted, the Ark being brought to Jerusalem represented a victory to David. It was a source of joy, something worth celebrating. He had sought the Lord; the Lord heard him; and he was delivered from his fears (Psalms 34:4). His appointment to rule over the Lord's people was also a blessing. Therefore, David danced and praised the Lord with all his might upon entering the city.

Despite being eternally heartbroken by the loss of my brother, I am thankful to God and find a sense of both joy and peace in the fact that we had 30 loving years together, creating memories that will last a lifetime. And just like David, I sought the Lord; He heard me; and delivered me from that dark place I was once in. This was something I alone nor anyone else could have done.

Although I know I will be coping with the loss of my brother for the rest of my life, having grown spiritually throughout the process represents a victory to me. It is another source of joy, something worth celebrating, and yet another reason to give Him praise.

- **"My Story is My Testimony"**

When David returned home and was confronted by his wife, Michal, he shared his story – his testimony – with her. He detailed how God had chosen him, despite his flaws, mistakes, and issues, to rule over His people. And as an expression of gratitude, he would continue to unapologetically dance and give Him praise.

Pastor Curney also shed light on the fact that when Michal saw David dancing from the window, she judged him – despite not knowing his story or the reason behind his actions or praise. Pastor Curney continued by acknowledging this as something we as Christians are often guilty of: judging the actions of others, not knowing what God has taken (or is taking) them through or what cross they have been asked to bear. In other words, not knowing their story.

This book is my story and my testimony. And it is only by the grace of God that I am able to share it with you. I know, for certain, that God has and will continue to carry me through this grieving process. And for that, I am grateful and will forever give Him praise.

I am also no longer concerned with how others view my actions (or lack thereof) during this grievous period or the praise that I express as a result of my testimony. Because more than likely, if you are judging me – *"you don't know my story."*

"Oprah's Master Class: Dwayne 'The Rock' Johnson"

During the initial two weeks of my cocoon phase, I began watching episodes of *Oprah's Master Class* on her television network, *OWN*. I had watched several episodes prior to watching the one featuring Dwayne "The Rock" Johnson, yet, none of them moved me the way this particular episode did.

I remember crying as I watched it. I could see so much of myself and my current situation as The Rock was discussing the obstacles and challenges he faced and dealt with in his life. I ended up watching the episode several times, and each time I found myself almost as emotional as I had been originally. However, I received the most benefit from the episode upon watching it for the second time (immediately after the situation with my supervisor).

For those of you who have never watched *Oprah's Master Class,* I want to provide a brief description of the show: Certain celebrities or influential people, whom Oprah refers to as "masters" of their craft by the end of the show, are interviewed about their life story and road to success. They each discuss the positive and negative experiences that ultimately allowed them to reach their current position or status.

Each experience is preceded by words of advice, inspiration, or encouragement from the master being interviewed. You can think of these words as key, or takeaway, points from the episode. I like to think of them as little life jewels (and that is how I will refer to them from here on out).

Now, to be honest, I could probably write an entire book elaborating on the jewels and experiences that The Rock shares in his episode. For now, however, I will only discuss those that pertain to coping with the loss of my brother or my experiences during this time.

- **Take Nothing for Granted**

When explaining the experience that taught him this jewel, The Rock describes a potentially tragic incident involving his mother. Although the incident's ending was ultimately or somewhat happy, it made him realize *"how precious life is and how in an instant, it could all go away."* So, you should take nothing for granted.

Jason's passing taught me this lesson. Up until April 29, 2017, phrases like *"Life's too short,"* and, *"Tomorrow's not promised,"* were somewhat cliché to me – just to be completely honest. But on that day, those phrases became facts. Because although I know my God makes no mistakes, I still feel like Jason's life was way too short, and his seemingly untimely passing proved tomorrow *definitely* isn't promised.

Even though I have no regrets about the relationship I had with my brother during his 30 years of life (we were closer than most, especially opposite sex, siblings, and I know he was aware of how much I loved him and vice versa), his passing taught me to take nothing in this life for granted.

It put things into perspective for me, reminding me to spend time with the people I love; to tell people I love them; to laugh as much I can; to apologize when I'm wrong; to be the bigger person sometimes; to forgive people; to not hold grudges; but most importantly – to live. Because, like The Rock said, in an instant, it (or they) could be gone.

▪ **Listen to Your Gut**

The Rock's explanation or description of this jewel touched me in more than one way. He begins by describing how he felt after being cut from the Canadian Football League (CFL) at the age of 23 after not originally being drafted by the National Football League (NFL) here in the U.S. After the cut, he was forced to move back home with his parents, which ultimately left him in a state of deep depression.

He then went on to state: *"With depression, one of the most important things you can realize, is that you're not alone. You're not the first to go through it, and you're not gonna be the last to go through it. And often times [when] it happens you feel like you're alone…like it's only you, and you're in your bubble…"* This is exactly how I felt after losing Jason, especially during my cocoon phase. I felt helpless, hopeless – and alone.

The Rock then goes on to say: *"You've just gotta remember [to] hold on to that fundamental quality of faith. Have faith that, on the other side of your pain…is something good."* For me, those "good things" were, first and foremost, my newfound spiritual, mental, and emotional strength. Although my heart will forever be broken by the passing of my brother, I am thankful for the strength I have gained while coping with my loss.

The second good thing – well, great thing in my opinion – was this book. Jason always envisioned himself being famous one day, or at least very well known. And I was determined to make that dream come true for him, posthumously, by writing and publishing this book. Like I said, when I began writing it, I had no idea how or when it would be published. I just knew it would be.

The Rock continues this story by sharing the fact that about a month and a half after returning home to his parents, the CFL called him back to begin playing football again. But he decided not to return. Instead, he decided he wanted to join the [family] business of wrestling – despite the original opposition of his father, a former wrestler. The Rock understood his father's concerns, but in the end decided to follow his gut and wrestle. This turned out to be one of the best decisions in his life.

The aforementioned situation or scenario was similar to one of mine. When I initially told my mom I wanted to write a book about coping with my loss, although she didn't oppose the idea, she definitely had some doubts and reservations: *"Do you have that much to talk about?" "Are you going to have enough words or pages?" "Do you have any idea how to get published?"*

I certainly understood my mom's concerns. Hell, I had similar concerns myself. But like The Rock, I ultimately decided to follow my gut and write my book, in hopes of one day sharing my story with the world. This turned out to be one of the best decisions (and largest accomplishments) of my life as well.

- **Let Go of Your Grudges**

Although Jason's passing shed light on not holding grudges, The Rock described this jewel from a different angle: not holding grudges based on a person's *"ability to love."* To describe this, he uses the relationship he once had with his father versus the relationship the two of them have now.

His dad's father passed away when his dad was a young boy. The following year, his dad's mother began dating someone. Later, an incident occurred in which she had to choose between keeping her son (The Rock's dad) or keeping her new boyfriend in her home. She chose her boyfriend and kicked her son out, leaving The Rock's dad without a home at age thirteen.

The Rock then describes this as his dad's ability (or capacity) to love. This capacity was minimal because his dad had no real reference of love. In understanding the challenges his dad faced as a child, The Rock says, he now has a better relationship with his father. And the grudges he once held growing up, he no longer holds.

This applies to the initial feelings, or grudges, I held with my friends, family, and loved ones who disappointed me during my times of need. After hearing The Rock's perspective, I later realized that many of them probably did the best they could, based on not only their ability to love, but also their ability to provide additional care and support to someone in my position.

Furthermore, the reason their actions (or lack thereof) didn't meet my expectations is because our abilities to love or provide such care and support are different. This is not to say that my ability is right, and their ability is wrong. It just means that they are different. And this difference is more than likely based on the things that we may (or may not) have experienced in our lives. That being the case, my grudges have since (and more easily) lessened.

- **Find Your Anchor**

The Rock explains the origin of this jewel by sharing a story about him (age 14 at the time) and his mother. One day, the two of them came home to an eviction notice on their door. At this point, he felt his family had reached an all-time low. He remembered looking at his mom as she began to cry. Seeing her cry moved him in such a way that he promised himself he would do everything in his power to ensure he and his family were never evicted again.

He goes on to say that his interpretation of success, or men who "made it" at that time, were all men who were *physical* guys. Whether it was his real-life role models (such as his dad, who was a wrestler) or his onscreen idols (Harrison Ford, Clint Eastwood, etc.). These were all men who built their bodies.

So, every day, he'd go to the local Boys Club after school to work out, attempting to ensure his family was never evicted again. So, he'd never have to see his mother cry that way. That was his original motivation or drive. Training or physical activity has since become his anchor. It keeps him grounded. So much so, that it is now his daily goal or achievement.

Like The Rock, training or physical fitness is also my anchor. Even more so now with the passing of my brother. Jason and I were not only workout buddies, but also each other's biggest cheerleader, especially when it came to testing our physical strengths and abilities.

In his absence, I know he'd want me to continue pushing myself and my body to the next level. As a result, I am now stronger than I ever have been. And every time I hit a new max or PR, I can hear him clapping and cheering: *"That's what I'm talkin' 'bout Eb! That's what I'm talkin' bout! Wit' yo' buff a**!"* – lol.[*]

Secondly, working out – or, my anchor – allows me to totally disconnect from the outside world and focus on myself, with the added benefit of getting healthier. I leave my phone in a locker or in the car, so I have no distractions. The only things I may carry with me are water, a towel, and my iPod – in which I only listen to Erv's music. And albeit temporary, during my workouts, I am at peace, which is something you desperately long for when coping with such a loss.

- **Seize Your *"Seven Bucks Moment"***

When The Rock got cut from the CFL in 1995, he remembered having only "seven bucks" in his pocket. He had hit, what he considered to be, rock bottom. This was a critical moment in his life in which he had to *"scratch and claw at"* any and every opportunity that arose – regardless of how small – in the hopes of, one day, creating a bigger opportunity. Now, he and his brand or team (Seven Bucks Production) have grown tremendously, and he credits that growth to the belief, or notion, that: *"[If] it's an opportunity, we will take advantage of it – always."*

My *"seven bucks moment"* occurred after leaving the meeting with my supervisor on October 6, 2017. At that point, I had recently lost my one and only sibling (and best friend). And it seemed as if I was on the verge of losing my job as well, which would ultimately

---

[*] When strength training, a "max" is the maximum amount of weight you can lift – usually for a single repetition. PR = personal record.

mean losing everything. So, there I was: right back at rock bottom –
well, close. (My faith had been restored, and I was no longer angry at
God at this point.)

Although I won't go into detail here, that was the moment that
ultimately changed my life. The moment that created small
opportunities for me to *"scratch and claw at"* until a bigger
opportunity presented itself.

In summary, these two experiences, Pastor Curney's message
and *Oprah's Master Class* featuring The Rock, ultimately changed my
life by helping restore my spiritual, mental, and emotional strength and
toughness. Upon revisiting them, I felt empowered and ready to fight
the world. I finally broke free from the dark place that once covered
me (my cocoon) and stepped into my new life with confidence – like a
butterfly.

Faith *Over* Fear

Attending New Mercies with my mom essentially helped
restore my faith in God. As Pastor Curney suggested, I drew nearer to
Him. I began attending church once again on a routine basis. Always
taking something away from the message, attempting to become a
student of the scripture.

In addition, I began praying more often. Not only when I was
mourning Jason or in times of need, but also just to thank God for

everything He has done; everything He is currently doing; and everything He will continue to do in my life.

Despite my loss, my relationship with God is stronger than it has ever been. I finally realized and understood that the only way I was going to truly begin to heal and move forward in the right direction, was with His help, guidance, strength, and grace.

This is not to say that I won't continue to hurt or grieve the loss of my brother, because I know I will – until the day I die. And his seemingly untimely passing will *always* be beyond my understanding. Nonetheless, I am confident that my hard days will eventually be fewer and farther between. I am also confident that in between my hard days, there will be life. There will be good days. And I have no one to thank for that *but* God.

Family Ties

▪ The Three of Us

Even though our family dynamic will never be the same upon losing Jason, the bond between my parents and I is still very close. We may even be a tad bit closer in his absence. And although we opted to discontinue previous family traditions (like our annual summer cruise) and to not attend the Dallas vs. Atlanta football game in 2017, we decided that the three of us would begin a new annual tradition in the years to come.

Jason did quite a bit of traveling in his short span of adulthood. In addition to the places he visited often, such as Miami and New Orleans (Mardis Gras), there were several other events and places that he mentioned wanting to participate in or visit – for example, attending *The Taste of Chicago* and other food festivals; going to a Dallas football game; and visiting cities such as Las Vegas and New York.

My parents and I plan to begin visiting these cities and taking part in such events, carrying Erv along for the ride in our hearts (and on our bodies given our tattoos and all the paraphernalia we have, lol). Although it won't compare to having him there in the flesh, I know he will be with us in spirit and smiling down on us from Heaven. He'd be happy that we didn't allow his absence to stop us from doing things together as a family.

Medical Attention

Although I never sought the assistance of a psychiatrist or therapist, I eventually received additional medicinal support to help cope with my loss. I had originally been given Vistaril to help with my insomnia. However, over time it became less useful.

When I mentioned this to my doctor during my second appointment, he suggested that I try the (generic) drug trazodone. Trazodone is an antidepressant medication that is often prescribed solely to treat insomnia, as somnolence is the number one side effect of the drug. Therefore, my doctor thought it might be of dual benefit given my loss.

I was started on the lowest dose of trazodone. I filled the prescription right away, but I was hesitant to use it. Although I was still battling with insomnia, I didn't like the thought of being on antidepressant therapy. Nonetheless, I decided to give the medication a try considering the pros outweighed the cons:

It wasn't a controlled substance, so I didn't have to worry about dependence. Also, because the medicine was taken at bedtime, I would experience the benefits of the drug, without having to worry so much about potential side effects, as most of the drug would be cleared overnight while I was sleeping.

Additionally, since I was started on the lowest dose, if or when the current dose becomes ineffective, the dose could be increased (without increasing the risk of side effects). And finally, because trazodone is an antidepressant, like my doctor mentioned, it could be of dual benefit surrounding my loss.

My experience with trazodone thus far has been great. The lowest dose has been effective. I am now sleeping soundly and throughout the night. I also feel alert and well rested when I wake up (unlike other sleep aids, which often leave patients feeling sluggish or groggy the next morning).

Moreover, I have yet to experience any major or unpleasant side effects. To date (November 2017), however, it is difficult to determine the antidepressant benefit, as I have only been taking the medication for about a month now. Nonetheless, I am glad I decided to make use of the prescription.

Career Path and Interactions

During my medical leave, I decided to meet with my supervisor to make yet another attempt at stepping down from my pharmacy manager role. However, considering the incident that occurred during my previous meeting with him, I asked that he (the pharmacy supervisor) and his direct report (the district manager) both be present at the meeting. They both agreed, and the meeting was scheduled.

It is important to note that this was not the same district manager (DM) I met with during my initial six weeks off. She retired earlier that summer and was temporarily replaced with an interim DM. The DM that I would be meeting with, however, was her final replacement. Considering he had only held the position in my district for about month (if that long) before I went out on leave, I assumed he wouldn't know much of the history or details surrounding my situation.

Not wanting to leave anything to chance, I figured it would be best for me to begin the meeting by briefing the DM on the events that led to my need to meet with them. Because the subject matter was sensitive, however, I decided to type up everything I wanted to say. I didn't want to leave anything out if I were to become emotional. To my surprise, the DM was glad I had taken the time to prepare my thoughts and concerns beforehand.

I started by sharing the circumstances and details surrounding my loss. I then went on to discuss the original meeting I had with my supervisor and previous DM, owning the fact that I had asked to remain in my pharmacy manager role at that time. I followed with my concerns about remaining in the position upon my return to work. I then described my two failed attempts to step down from my management position and the incident that occurred at the previous meeting with my supervisor.

I concluded my speech by letting them know the date in which my doctor cleared me to return to work and the condition that he set forth upon my return: I was not to be scheduled for more than 32 hours per week for at least the next six months. I ended with a third attempt to step down from management.

I not only reiterated my concern with remaining in the position, but also assured them that I could still be an asset within the district in a lesser role. I also expressed my need *and* love for my job, making sure to mention my 12 years of service with the company.

The DM responded by first expressing his condolences for my loss. He then went on to say that he and my supervisor would have to contact human resources (HR) about the things in which I had discussed. Upon receiving feedback from HR, they would then be in contact with me. Since our meeting was on a Monday, they assured that I would hear from them before the week was out.

I ended up hearing from the DM and my supervisor via conference call that Friday. They informed me that I would be able to step down from management upon my return and discussed the conditions of my demotion. The seemingly most important condition or issue was the reduction in my hourly wage.

Considering the pay reduction wasn't by much, I was unbothered. (The difference in pay even further solidified that remaining in management was not worth the additional responsibility or stress.) They also would have no problem honoring my doctor's condition of a max of 32 hours per week for the next six months. Thus, allowing me to work a reduced work schedule throughout the holidays and surrounding the first anniversary of Jason's passing.

Ultimately, my prayers had been answered. I was able to step down; remain in my district; and work fewer hours around my foreseen difficult and emotional time periods. The only downside was that I would have to leave my current team, whom I had become so fond of. And not only would I be leaving them, but I'd be leaving abruptly, not returning to work at my store at all upon the conclusion of my leave.

I set up a final staff meeting to announce my departure. It ended up being a very emotional meeting. I hated to leave them. And although they understood why I was leaving, they hated to see me leave as well. Nonetheless, I had to do what was best for me.

Overall, I was thankful for the opportunity to step down. Due to the demotion, I knew I would be less stressed upon returning to work, ultimately resulting in a greater peace of mind and improved quality of life. I also felt the change in pharmacy scenery would be good for my healing process.[*]

The Gym and The Music

During my month away from work, I decided to stop shying away from the activities that once brought me joy or the activities that Erv and I used to do together. I fell back on my trusted anchor – the gym. Although I knew I wouldn't be able to spend as much time in the gym upon returning to work, I took full advantage while I had the time to spare.

I started back training with Caleb, taking his classes several times a week. I worked out or strength trained on my own several

---

[*] Interestingly enough, less than a month after I returned to work, my company announced changes to its upper level management structure. I suspect my supervisor did not get offered one of the new management positions because soon after the announcement, he put in his resignation and left the company by the end of the year (2017). I was instantly reminded of Pastor Curney's words: *"God will handle people when they mishandle you."* Amen!

times a week. And I took a yoga class at least once a week. I'd often end up doing two-a-days between the three activities. I also downloaded even more of Erv's music to my iPod. And anytime I worked out on my own, I'd still listen to his music and his music only.

It felt great to reconnect with my "gym family" after not working out with them for so long. Even though I was at my heaviest weight when I started back working out with Caleb, I never felt judged by any of my gym colleagues. The amount of love and support they showed upon my return and have continued to show has helped me more than they will ever know.

In addition to my consistent physical activity, I also cleaned up my diet during this time. I stopped using food as a source of comfort for my grief, because the end result of doing so (weight gain) was an additional source of grief, in and of itself. I still treat myself to pizza on a weekly basis and other foods I enjoy here and there. But, overall, I have a healthy relationship with food now.

With my diet now in check; my gym family's support; and my angel's encouragement and motivation from the Heavens above, I am confident I will not only lose the additional weight I gained during my grieving process but bounce back better than ever. Erv always said and believed I was more than capable of having my "dream body." Now, more than ever, I am determined to make that a reality.

Social Media

In addition to increasing my gym presence, I also began increasing my social media presence once again. Although I don't post nearly as often as I did immediately following Jason's passing (primarily because I don't have as much time to spare between writing and working out), I still try to make it a point to post something on Instagram at least once or twice a week and Facebook at least a few times each month.

In addition to Instagram and Facebook, I also decided to become active on Twitter once again, after not posting a tweet in over four years! I must admit, at the time of writing this, I am still getting used to Twitter. As one would imagine, a lot has changed about the app since I was last active. However, I can confidently say I at least have the "tweeting" part down. That will suffice for now.

I am still beyond thankful for social media. Between my three accounts, I can always find something to uplift me, motivate or encourage me, or make me smile or laugh. Social media also continues to be an outlet for me to express my grief without tears. Lastly, it will forever be a means for me to honor Erv's memory and legacy.

Tattoos and Paraphernalia

Although I have yet to get any additional tattoos, I *have* gotten some additional "Erv paraphernalia" since my original grieving period. At this point, I'm sure you're saying to yourself: *"She already has t-shirts, wristbands, and buttons. What else could she possibly have!?"* The answer: jewelry and car décor.

The first piece of jewelry I received as a gift at my birthday, or celebration of [Erv's] life, event. Three of my friends went in on a sterling silver Pandora charm bracelet. It was so thoughtful. They purchased a chef hat charm and had the words *"family forever"* engraved on the bracelet itself.

I later purchased two additional charms: a crown and a circular charm that reads *"family forever."* Because the bracelet is so nice, however, I reserve it for church on Sundays and other outings or events in which I am dressed up. (Otherwise, I wear one or both of my elastic wristbands.)

The second piece of jewelry I have is a sterling silver necklace containing a *"30 years of love"* charm, also from Pandora. The charm is heart-shaped, with a rhinestone-covered number 30 in the center. I've worn the necklace every day since I purchased it. I love the way it perfectly sums up the relationship I had with my brother – 30 years of love. And the relationship we had during those 30 years will forever be held sacred in my heart.

The final piece of jewelry is a combination of rings. My mom gave me two silver rings, one with my name engraved on it and the other with Jason's. I wear these two rings along with a small sapphire ring (our birthstone) on the middle finger of my left hand. *(Hopefully, someone will put a ring on the adjacent finger before I go on to meet Jason.)*

For my 33rd birthday (2017), I decided to upgrade my BMW to the 2018 model. Upon purchasing the car, I decided I wanted to have my license plate personalized in memory of Erv. However, I couldn't come up with anything I liked within the 7-character restriction. So, I decided to get a customized frame instead.

Luckily, I was able to find a personalized frame kit at my local Auto Zone. The kit included a matte black plastic frame and a combination of 100+ capital letters, numbers, spaces, and icons. I could put exactly what I wanted on the frame: "LONG LIVE KING ERV." I put "LONG LIVE on the top portion of the frame and "KING

ERV" on the bottom. I also put a cross icon to the left of the word "KING" and a heart icon to the right of the word "ERV."

The finished product turned out great. I ended up getting several compliments from people who knew me and Erv. In fact, I was almost as proud (if not more) of the frame as I was the new car!

Social Interactions

Although I didn't take much of Jason's advice about getting out and being more social while he was here, in his absence, I have decided to finally listen. I'm going to make every effort to simply *live more*. Now, I'm not saying I plan to start hitting the club, getting sections, and buying bottles like he would've done if he were me. But I am going to try my best to begin living my life to the fullest and with no regrets. Just like he did.

During my free time, I plan to start doing more of the things I enjoy and traveling to places I've always wanted to visit. My first goal, however, is to make it a priority to simply slow down and to not always be so "busy." That way, I'll at least have the energy needed to do these things. (Thankfully, my demotion to staff pharmacist will also allow more room for this.)

Additionally, I am going to make a conscious effort to begin focusing my time and energy on the people I love and those who make a sincere effort to be a part of my life, letting go of the ones who make no such effort. I want (and need) to protect my energy as best I can. I recognize that hanging on to certain friendships and relationships may not be best for me, especially during this difficult time in my life. So, I must act accordingly.

Two of the many things Jason's passing solidified for me are 1) that our time on Earth is precious, and 2) it can all be over within the blink of an eye. Therefore, my optimum goal is to surround myself with people who care about my well-being and have my best interest at heart. All while living the happiest, most fulfilled, and ultimately, the best life I possibly can. In essence, I simply want to *live, love, and laugh* with good people. Just as my angel often did.

Dating and Relationships

When it came to the men I chose to date, Jason often criticized me for putting up with less than I deserve. He often accused me of not seeing my own worth. I remember he once said: *"Eb, you too good for this sh*t dawg (shaking his head). I'm tellin' you, these dudes takin' you for granted! Let me find a girl who's half the woman you are. Man, I promise I'd be doing everything in my power to do right by her!"* And just like almost everything else, Erv was right.

Now, contrary to Erv's belief, I always knew my worth. The problem was: I didn't always act like it. However, upon Erv's passing, my mindset changed – drastically. This is not to say that I began acting stuck-up, rude, or cold-hearted when it came to finding love, because I didn't. It simply meant that, because I knew what I "brought to the table," I was no longer afraid of "eating alone" until someone matched my efforts.

I had already developed an *"everyone is dispensable"* mentality upon losing Jason. And when it came to dating and relationships, I developed an additional mindset: *"You either come correct or leave me be."* It was just that simple.

I no longer had the energy to continue repeating different failed scenarios, *especially* with men from my past. In fact, upon Erv's passing, I felt as though tolerating anything less than what I deserved would be a disgrace to him. And considering I've wanted to do nothing but honor my brother in his absence, I refused to continue acting as if I wasn't worth a man's best effort.

Additionally, given my newly restored faith in God and His timing, I can honestly say that I am content being single at the moment. I take pride in being able to say this given the negative stigma society has placed on 30+ year-old single or childless women. (I could probably write a book about that too.)

Nonetheless, I am confident that *"one day my prince will come"* and that he and I will have at least one child, whom we will name Jason. Even if we are blessed with a little girl, her name will be Jason. We'll just call her *Jacy*. Having said this, if you are reading this excerpt as my future husband or someone who knows me personally, please understand, this name is not up for debate.

Rainbows and The Supernatural

Although I continued to see rainbows on many of my most difficult or emotional days, I eventually began seeing them less and less. Seeing fewer rainbows implied that my hard days and times were becoming fewer and farther between, signifying that I had indeed begun to heal. In essence, this was an answer to my prayers.

However, even though the rainbows became less present, Erv's spirit did not. In fact, as time went on, it seemed as though his spirit became more and more vocal. Not only did I hear from him more often, but I'd also hear from him regardless of my circumstance or condition: on good days, on bad days, at home, at church, in the car, at the gym, at the store, even in the bathroom. Literally, any- and everywhere.

But I welcomed Erv's spirit. It was always a source of laughter, motivation, encouragement, wisdom, advice, and tough love. Just as his presence had always been in the flesh.

In addition to Erv's spirit being more vocal, I also feel as though part of his spirit actively dwells in me, giving me a newfound strength and confidence. In Erv's absence, I was no longer afraid to speak up for myself and actively seek the things I wanted and deserved – in all aspects of my life.

In a way, it was like we once again reverted to our childhood ways, in which I was more vocal to the world, while Jason (or his spirit) only spoke to me. To be completely honest, I also developed a bit of his potty mouth. But I'm working on that.

In hindsight, Jason's spirit being more vocal once I began feeling a little better made perfect sense. When he was alive, Erv always tended to avoid me when I was feeling down or depressed, making contact only when necessary. But when I was in good spirits, it seemed as if he was always around or hanging out with me. Obviously, the same is true in his absence.

Celebration of Life

Going forward, I decided I would no longer be hosting any birthday parties for myself or to celebrate Erv's life. Given the amount of time and energy I put into the last one and the emotional distress that later ensued, I figured it was probably best not to make that a tradition.

Although, at the time of writing this, I haven't decided what my new birthday tradition will be, I know two things for sure: 1) I will *always* take time away from work to celebrate our birthdays, and 2) In Erv's memory, the celebration will *always* involve pizza, a long island iced tea, and a slice of cake from Publix (one of Erv's favorite desserts).

I always admired Erv's mental and emotional strength, as well as, his tenacity to chase his dreams; go for what he felt he deserved; and to simply live his life the way HE wanted to live it – without any regrets nor seeking the validation of others. With that in mind, I've concluded that, ultimately, the best way I can celebrate my brother's life and legacy, is to do the same in his absence – to live…to *unapologetically*…LIVE.

CONCLUSION

If you've ever suffered the loss of a sibling, it is my hope, upon reading this book – a story of my experiences and insight – that you have gained some assistance in coping with your loss. Alternatively, if you have not experienced such loss but know someone who has, I hope you have gained some understanding of what that person may be going through and how you can best help them during their time of need.

Coping with the loss of a sibling entails coping with a loss of both the past and the future. The memories associated with the past may be an initial source of grief but will hopefully serve to bring you a sense of peace, contentment, or happiness when you look back on them. The circumstances of the present may stir up feelings of both joy and pain. Although you can't erase any of the painful events that may have occurred, choose to focus on the ones that bring you the most joy.

The aspects of your loved one's passing may be almost unbearable to relive or replay in your mind, but they are a part of your story. And the fact that you lived through them, speaks to your strength. Lastly, although the realities of the future may be difficult to accept in the beginning, ironically, the most difficult of these – the fact that life goes on – is also the most promising, so try your hardest to find comfort in that.

Never in my wildest dreams – or worst nightmares – did I envision living my life without my brother, Jason, especially at the tender age of 32. Thus, having to cope and learn to live with such an eternal pain. However, despite being the most broken I have ever been, I can coincidentally (and confidently) say, I am also the strongest I have ever been – physically, mentally, emotionally, and spiritually – and for that, I am thankful.

EPILOGUE: It's Never Too Late

*"It has been said 'time heals all wounds.' I do not agree.
The wounds remain. In time, the mind – protecting its sanity –
covers them with scar tissue, and the pain lessens.
But it is never gone."*
– Rose Kennedy

Around the second anniversary of Jason's passing, I went into another deep depression and heavy grieving period. There were several contributing factors, but the primary factor was my job. My pharmacist partner (the pharmacy manager) had taken a leave of absence for a little over three months prior to the anniversary. And guess who had to act as interim manager during that time? Me.

Serving as pharmacy manager presented several challenges. The increased workload resulted in me spending additional time at the pharmacy to complete tasks, and, at times, making myself available outside of work for questions, concerns, conference calls, etc. Thus, leaving me with less time and energy for myself and the things I enjoy.

Additionally, the last time I held the position with any vigor, my brother was alive. So, being thrust back into the pharmacy manager role was also rough on me emotionally. I was reminded of all the events, both good and bad, that occurred when I originally held the role. So, not only was I significantly more stressed, but my grief was also exacerbated during this period.

Everything seemed so much harder during this time. Getting out of bed each morning was harder. Falling (and staying) asleep at night was harder. Taking care of myself was harder. Going to work and being productive was harder. Focusing on my goals was harder. Wearing a smile was harder. Holding back tears was harder. Praying and remaining faithful was harder. LIFE in and of itself – was harder.

By the time the month of April arrived, I was in a state of full-blown depression. And as the anniversary (the 29th) approached, my grief only got heavier. I thought once I got past the anniversary, I would begin to feel a little better emotionally, but I didn't. In fact, I began feeling worse. I ultimately experienced a mental health crisis and had to seek medical attention, scheduling an emergency appointment with my physician. He ordered that I take a medical leave of absence from work for a period of at least one month.

Although I still did not begin any new or additional antidepressant therapy in the time leading up to my crisis, I did begin taking the trazodone I had been prescribed on a routine basis (every night) versus only when needed. Taking the trazodone every night didn't necessarily help with my mood or grief. But it did help me rest well most nights, which at least gave me the strength to function a little better each day.

During my time off, however, I *did* begin going to therapy – something I *never* thought I would do. (If you recall, I mentioned my reservations about therapy in *Chapter 9: The Grief.*) But at this point, I had reached another all-time low with my grief and depression. I had also begun experiencing frequent panic (anxiety) attacks once again.

My ability to cope with everything on my own had diminished. And since I refused any supportive medicinal therapy, I finally decided to give psychotherapy a try. I wasn't sure if it would help, but I figured it couldn't hurt.

Starting therapy was probably one of the best decisions I could have made during that time (and in general). The help, relief, and support my therapist has provided was the answer to a prayer – the missing piece of my mental health puzzle.

In therapy, I am receiving the blueprint for managing my depression while coping with my loss. I am also learning more about who I am and the person I am becoming. I look forward to each session and feel better and stronger after each one. I almost regret not seeking help sooner.

Everyone's personal grief reaction or experiences upon losing a sibling, or any loved one, will be different. But for all of us, one thing holds true: The grief in our hearts will last a lifetime. With time, the pain and our expressions of grief may lessen, but it will never completely go away. The grief for our loved one(s) is eternal, ultimately lasting until the day we die ourselves.

That being the case, please understand that it's *never* too late (or too early) to seek the help you need to cope with your loss – whether it be medicinal therapy, psychotherapy, joining a support group, or spiritual guidance. Know that you can benefit from any or all these things at any point in your grief journey. Don't be afraid or ashamed to take the steps necessary to help you begin living your best life despite your loss.

You are going to miss and grieve your loved one(s) forever. But I'm sure he or she wouldn't want you to suffer any harder or for any longer than you have to in their absence. I know my angel is proud I took that next step and started therapy, getting the help I desperately needed. I'm sure yours will be too.

Additionally, if you are reading this passage as someone who knows someone who lost a sibling (or any loved one), understand that it's never too late to express your condolences, to show acts of sympathy, or to simply reach out and check on that person given their loss.

Regardless of how much time has passed, that person *still* has some level of hurt in their heart. That person *still* has very hard and challenging days each year due to their loss (birthdays, holidays, and anniversaries to name a few). So, that person could *still* use your love and support.

Thank you so much for reading for my story. If you have recently lost a sibling, or any loved one, I pray for your strength and God's peace when you need it most. Be blessed. Take care. And remember, it's never too late...

ACKNOWLEDGMENTS

First and foremost, I must thank God for being a source of continued strength throughout this difficult grieving process. I know, without a shadow of a doubt, I wouldn't have made it this far without His help and guidance along the way. I'd also like to thank Him for the ability to finish this book – my story about coping with the loss of my beloved brother, Jason. My very first tattoo was *"Phil[ippians] 4:13."* Being a first-time author, this book is yet another testimony that: *"I can do all things through Christ who strengthens me."*

I'd like to thank my parents, Ronnie and Sarah Grays Ervin, for raising Jason and I the way in which you did – teaching us to love each other not only as siblings, but also as best friends. You two are the reason our sibling bond was so strong, and for that I am beyond grateful. I also want to thank you for all the time the four of us spent together as a family, creating memories that will supersede time and remain in our hearts until we see Jason again. Lastly, I'd simply like to thank you for the unconditional love, care, guidance, and support you've showered us with our entire lives. It was your teaching and examples of these traits that molded us into the adults we became. Adults that you could be proud of. WE love you.

I would also like to thank my extended family for your love and support during this time. Special thanks to my cousins (Shantel, Kris, Jennifer, Morgan, Mackenzie, La'Darius, Tavaris, Tiffany, and Tammara) for your continued expressions of love, concern, and support. Your increased presence during my times of need made me so much stronger, and your ability to make me laugh despite my pain will always be remembered and appreciated.

Alex, Erica, and Katrenia, I am so glad to call you all my best friends. We've known each other since grade school, and I'm thankful that our friendship has not only lasted over the years, but has managed to grow even stronger. Thank you for always showing your love and support on both my good and bad days, but especially on the bad ones. I value your friendship more than you'll ever know and look forward to many more fun times in the future.

Hope and Adriene, even though I met you girls later in life (college and pharmacy school, respectively), I feel like I've known the two of you forever. I'm so thankful our friendship lasted beyond the classroom. And although life keeps us too busy to talk on a regular basis, I cherish and enjoy every minute of our hour-plus "catch-up" phone sessions, lol.

To the other friends I have made growing up, in school, or after (Bam, BJ, Chris, Darrell, Derrick, Fred, La'Britney, Lyndrick, *Roommate*, She'Nae, *Teammate*, and Tornica) as well as to Jason's friends whom I can now call my friends (Reu, Matt, Devon, A.J., *Jiffy*, Mary, La'Quena, Tyrone, and Tyson) – thank you. Even though we may not communicate very often (or much at all anymore), just know I greatly appreciate the love, support, and encouraging words you provided during my time of need. And regardless of the current status of our friendship, I am so thankful our paths crossed.

To my work family, thank you for accepting me (and Jason, lol) into your lives and hearts. Special thanks to the people who started out as coworkers that I can now call my friends: Fallon, Alana, Brian, Jewell, Ryan, Jazz, Tucker, Sara, Anna, Kay, Whit, Sirena,

Blaire, Eli, Shayy, Dionte, Brandi, Rodney, and NG. The extra love and support you guys showed when Jason passed will always be remembered and appreciated. To those of you I worked with during that time, thank you for making my shifts more bearable. I'd also like to thank my supervisor during that time for allowing the Devil to utilize him, in such a way, that ultimately created bigger blessings and opportunities for me. Thus, putting me in a better position to testify and glorify the power of my God.

To my "gym family" both old and new – thank you, thank you, thank you. With Jason and I living alone in Atlanta, you all were a huge source of strength and support for me surrounding his passing. I never felt alone when I was around or at the gym with you all. Your thoughts, prayers, and acts of kindness during that time will never be forgotten. I am also so thankful for the friendships and relationships I have been able to build with you all over the years. Joining the gym was definitely one of the best decisions I ever made.

To Pastor Snodgrass (rest in peace) and the members of Progressive Union Missionary Baptist Church – thank you. Pastor Snodgrass, thank you for laying my and Jason's spiritual foundation, ultimately leading us to give our lives to Christ and become saved and baptized. I'd also like to thank you for the words of comfort spoken at Jason's funeral. Special thanks also to Marques McDonald for the beautiful solo and any other members who played an active role or took part in the funeral preparation, service, or repass.

To Pastor Curney and the members of New Mercies Christian Church – thank you. Pastor Curney, thank you for allowing Jason and I into your heart and prayers. The amount of love and support shown by you and New Mercies during Jason's passing was incredible.

Special thanks to you for also allowing God to use you in such a way that ultimately got me back on the correct spiritual track.

To the Sorors of the Epsilon Eta Chapter of Delta Sigma Theta Sorority, Inc., and especially to my line sisters (Spring 2004) – thank you for your love and support during my difficult time. Despite the fact we all pretty much went our separate ways upon graduation, it still warms my heart to know that we still can (and will) always come together to support a Soror in need. True sisterhood.

To Darlene, Kim, Vivian, and the rest of my neighbors – thank you so much for watching over me, Jason, and our home, especially when we didn't realize you were doing so. I am so glad God saw fit for us to not only move into this neighborhood, but on our street in particular. I'd also like to thank you all for coming together and providing such kind words and wonderful acts of sympathy during my difficult time. You all went above and beyond to help a neighbor in need. And for that, I am grateful.

Kashima (The Social Hostess, LLC), thank you so much for helping host and plan my two birthday events in 2016 and 2017. You were the best party hostess/planner I could've asked for. Always so sweet and professional. Thanks to you, everything was beautiful and ran smoothly each year. Special thanks for the love and support you showed surrounding the 2017 event. Thank you for not only being a planner and hostess, but also a friend.

Dr. Parrott and Dr. Gibbs of the (former) Dekalb Medical Physicians Group, thank you for being two of the best physicians I could ask for. I appreciate your listening ears and willingness to provide whatever medical attention I needed to best manage everything I experienced surrounding the loss of my brother. Your expressions of sympathy and genuine care will be remembered for years to come – thank you.

Jay Peabody of The Peabody Practice, LLC. – thank you for helping me on my journey to better mental health. I thank God I found you when I did. I couldn't have asked for a better therapist. I know I had my initial reservations, but you were patient, understanding, and, ultimately, pushed me to become a better version of myself. For that, I am most grateful.

Special thanks to Royal Funeral Home; Valhalla Memory Gardens; Adam and Kristi of Kreations Tattoos & Body Piercing; Vance of Timeline Clothing; Tornica of Cakes by the Pound and More; Clara Toney; Dominique "DJ Immature" Nixon; Charlene Holden; Gloria Ayers and to *any-* and *everyone* else who supported me and my family surrounding Jason's passing – whether it was by attending his funeral; sending cards and messages filled with love, sympathy, and kind words; sending flowers or other gifts of love and support; keeping us in your thoughts and prayers; visiting us at our homes; being a listening ear or a shoulder to cry on; attending my birthday/celebration of life event; and any other act of sympathy or effort made to support us – thank you.

Lastly, but certainly not least, I have to thank my brother, my best friend, and now – my angel: Jason Tremaine Ervin. Erv, I love and miss you so much. Not a single day goes by where I don't think about you. Although I still feel like your time here on Earth was way too short, I am so thankful for the 30 years we had together and the unbreakable bond we had.

Thank you for always cheering me on and supporting me in my endeavors, regardless of how big or small. Thank you for your advice (both solicited and unsolicited) and for always being honest and upfront with me, even when I didn't want to hear it. If it needed to be said, you made it a point to say it. And I'm grateful for that.

Thank you for always being a judgment-free listening ear or a shoulder to cry on when I needed it. Thank you for the memories of love and laughter that you left behind. Those are the things that get me through my most difficult days. Thank you for leaving behind your music – a medium that transcends time, allowing me to still hear your voice and feel your personality each and every day.

In your absence, I want to thank you for my newfound strength – physical, mental, emotional, and spiritual – as I am stronger now than I have ever been. Thank you for all the rainbows that have appeared during my darkest days, instantly giving me a sense of peace when I needed it most. I hope you continue to make your presence known through these beautiful acts of nature.

Thank you for your continued protection and the additional sense of comfort and security I have because of it. Thank you for still motivating and cheering me on, giving advice, listening, and making me laugh from the Heavens above. I hope your spirit continues to be vocal and never leaves my side. In summary, thank you for not only being the best brother I could have, but also my best friend. Rest easy My Angel – until we meet again.

Love always, Eb.

P.S.   Erv, when I said you should be prepared to leave the house at age 30 – boy, you KNOW I didn't mean like that! –xoxo

ABOUT THE AUTHOR

Dr. Ebony N. Ervin was born and raised with her younger brother, Chef Jason Ervin, in Huntsville, AL. In 2006, she graduated from Stillman College (Tuscaloosa, AL) with a Bachelor of Science in Mathematics. She later received her Doctor of Pharmacy from Mercer University's College of Pharmacy & Health Sciences (Atlanta, GA) in 2010. She currently resides in Stone Mountain, GA and is practicing pharmacy at a major retail chain.

Upon losing Jason, Ebony also launched a personal blog site, DrEbSays.com, where she serves as an *unofficial* online life coach. On her website, Ebony shares her personal experiences and struggles with grief, mental health, conflict resolution, dating and relationships, spirituality, and everything in between. Through her candid transparency, Ebony is able to motivate, encourage, and inspire hundreds of people each week.

When Ebony is not writing or practicing pharmacy, she enjoys reading, working out, teaching spin (cycling) classes, spending time with friends and family, and being of service to those in need.

CONNECT WITH THE AUTHOR

- ❖ **Dr. Ebony N. Ervin**

    - Email: ebony.ervin_mbk@yahoo.com
    - Facebook: Ebony N. Ervin
    - Instagram | Twitter: @eb_erv

- ❖ **DrEbSays.com**

    - Email: DrEb@drebsays.com
    - Facebook | Instagram | Twitter: @drebsays

- ❖ *My Brother's Keeper*

    - Permissions: permissions_mbk@yahoo.com
    - DrEbSays.com/mbk

JASON TREMAINE ERVIN

September 10, 1986 – April 29, 2017

#LongLiveKingErv

Made in the USA
Columbia, SC
31 August 2019